THE
Enlightened
MARRIAGE

The 5 Transformative Stages of
Relationships and Why the Best Is
Still to Come

JED DIAMOND, PhD

The Enlightened Marriage
Edited by Patricia Kot
Typeset by PerfectType, Nashville, Tenn.
Cover design by Frame 25 Productions
Printed in the U.S.A.

To order this title, please call toll-free 1-800-CAREER-1 (NJ and Canada: 201-848-0310) to order using VISA or MasterCard, or for further information on books from Career Press.

The Career Press, Inc.
12 Parish Drive
Wayne, NJ 07470
www.careerpress.com

Library of Congress Cataloging-in-Publication Data

CIP Data Available Upon Request.

DEDICATION

I dedicate this book to my wife, Carlin,
who continues to teach me the meaning of real,
lasting love, and to all my clients over the last fifty years
who have trusted me to help them find real, lasting love.

CONTENTS

INTRODUCTION

I don't love you anymore. I'm not sure I ever did. I'm moving out. The kids will understand." When Laura Munson heard these words from her husband of twenty years, she did a very strange thing. She didn't cry. She didn't protest. She didn't fight back. She simply decided not to believe him. She made a commitment to "us" and refused to let her husband's midlife changes destroy what they had built together. She wrote about her experiences in a *New York Times* article, "Those Aren't Fighting Words."

In more than forty years counseling men and women, I've found that too many relationships end when they could be saved. There are certainly some couples that should not be together and when one person leaves it's a blessing for both, but most couples just don't know how to make a marriage that works for both partners and lasts a lifetime. Though the book focuses on heterosexual relationships, many of the same issues apply to couples and individuals regardless of their sexual orientation. We all have in common the desire to love and be loved. We'd all like to have an enlightened marriage that we create with a partner and lasts through time.

This is a book for you if you're interested in real, lasting love. I believe that most human beings want to be part of a pair, yet too many relationships fall apart. We lick our wounds and vow "never again," but loneliness and desire pull us back in, and once again we find ourselves reaching out to find a partner. However, even when we find that "special someone" we often live in fear that we'll lose them. Meanwhile, we face a world that seems to be pulling apart at the seams. Worries about violence at home and abroad, environmental disasters, and economic uncertainty, create added stress that can destabilize even the most solid relationships.

We don't have to be victims of the world around us. Even if our spouse is feeling down about the relationship, I've found that one person can do a lot to turn things around. Midlife can be the best time to be married. We are not so caught up with children and work. It's a time we can really enjoy each other and be true partners as we age. "Grow old along with me! The best is yet to be." These words by the poet Robert Browning capture what a lot of us long for as we move into midlife and beyond. However, as a marriage and family counselor I see too many relationships fall apart, just when the couple could be enjoying their lives the most. I see too many people that want to start again, but they are afraid of what they might face.

A recent research study found that the divorce rate among adults aged fifty and older doubled between 1990 and 2010. In 1990, one in ten people who got divorced were over fifty. Roughly one in four divorces in 2010 occurred to persons aged fifty and older. The study found that more than 600,000 people aged fifty and older got divorced in 2010, and they predict that the number of over-50 divorces in 2030, based on current trends, could easily top 800,000 per year. I've found that most midlife couples would rather stay together, but they don't know how to make things work, and those who would like to find a partner are afraid of making the same mistakes again.

I've written this book because I believe I've found the keys to having a long-term, successful relationship. I've been helping men, women, and couples for more than forty years. Though things can look bleak, I have great hope for the future. When I was discouraged about the state of the world, I wondered, "How can we possibly solve the world's problems if we can't even keep a couple's love alive?" Now, I feel the reverse may be true. If we can figure out how to have a joyful marriage that gets better as we age, maybe we can use *the Power of Two* to resolve the many problems in the world that threaten our survival.

Like everyone else on the face of the planet, I've wanted real, lasting love. And like everyone on the face of the planet I have not found these simple words—*Real, Lasting, Love*—easy to attain. Like many, I got married in my twenties. Being young and in love, we were sure our relationship would last a lifetime. It lasted ten years and produced two wonderful children. I fell in love again, but that relationship was short lived. Before giving it another try I vowed that I would figure out the secrets of having a relationship that lasted a lifetime.

I feel I've learned how to be joyfully in love and want to share what I've learned with you. My third marriage, to my wife, Carlin, is going strong after thirty-six years. We certainly have our ups and downs, but we've learned that most marriages can be revitalized and given new life. Whether your marriage is on the rocks, or it's good and you'd like it to be great, you can benefit from what you'll learn in this book. If you're single, but still believe in love and want a marriage that lasts, there is hope for you as well.

I'll be with you every step of the way. I may not know you personally, yet, but I care about you. I want you to have all the love you've always dreamed of having. I've written this book just for you, and I imagine that we're sitting together sharing our hopes and dreams. I've **bolded** parts that I want to emphasize, and I've given you specific steps to follow to help you get from where you are now to where you want to be. I've also summarized what

I've said so it will be easy for you to remember. If you have questions along the way you can contact me through my website: *www.MenAlive.com*. You can trust there's a real person here, and I'm looking forward to taking this journey with you. Let's begin.

One

The Five Stages of Marriage and Why Too Many Stop at Stage 3

*M*arcia was devastated when her husband of twenty-five years told her, "I'm not *in love* with you anymore. The life has gone out of our marriage, and I don't think we can get it back." Two days later her husband, Mark, moved out of the house. He said he needed to sort things out. The couple's two children were confused and afraid.

Marcia called me in full panic mode. "I feel blind-sided," she told me. "We've had our ups and downs, and Mark's been having a tough time with huge stresses at work, but I never thought it would come to this." After telling me about their lives up until now, Marcia broke into tears. "I love Mark and I don't want our marriage to end. What can I do?"

I told her that hearing the words "I'm not in love with you anymore" feels like having your heart ripped out. You think your world is collapsing. But it doesn't have to be the end. In fact, it may be just the beginning of a whole new relationship with the person you're with.

This is not just a problem for women. Many men who contact me as well. "My wife and I have been married for twenty-three years and it is like we are strangers," said Roy. "She has been saying that she isn't happy and she wants a divorce. She says she doesn't want to live the remainder of her life being unhappy. She has found interests that don't include me and says she has finally discovered that she only needs herself to be happy. There is no intimacy or affection; nor is there any fighting. We are coexisting. Please help."

Because you're reading this book I know you're interested in real, lasting love. You may be in a relationship that is wonderful already, but you want "wonderful" to last. Or you may be in a relationship that is anything but wonderful. Your relationship may be miserable, with constant fights, or it may be miserable with silent accusations and disappointments. The relationship may be in deep trouble, but you're not ready to give up and you're looking for answers. Finally, you may not be in a relationship now, but would like to be. You've probably been disappointed in the past, yet you hunger for real, lasting love.

Whatever your situation, know that you are not alone. I'm sure you are aware that there are millions of people who have experienced what you're experiencing now. I'm sure you know some of them personally. If we're over the age of fourteen, we've all had experiences of love that started off with great promise, but ended up in heartbreak. Most of us have had experience looking for love in all the wrong places.

It's said that we teach what we want to learn. For more than forty years I've been teaching people how to have successful marriages that remain passionate, loving, and creative through the years. Being a marriage and family counselor has been a satisfying career and I've helped thousands of couples. But the truth is my initial motivation for going into the field was to learn how I could have a successful marriage myself.

My parents divorced when I was five years old and I grew up being raised by a single mom. I vowed that what happened to them wouldn't happen to me. "When I fall in love, it would be forever." I probably remembered that from one of the love songs I heard growing up. "Forever" lasted almost ten years for me. I remarried and my second marriage lasted just two years. Before I married again, if I ever found the right person, I vowed I would learn the secret of real, lasting love.

My wife, Carlin, and I have now been married for thirty-six years. I'll tell you truthfully that it's been a struggle at times, and there were periods that we just seemed stuck in reverse and couldn't seem to move ahead in a positive way. But I can tell you, we've learned the secret of having a functional, joyful marriage. Learning about the five stages of marriage turned out to be the key to our success.

I still remember falling in love with Carlin. We met at an Aikido dojo and later reconnected at a weekend workshop, *Sex, Love, and Relationships.* I don't remember much of the formal learning because I was entranced with Carlin. We talked, walked on the beach, talked some more. I felt I had finally found my soul partner. We laughed together, played together, made mad, passionate love. Having finally found "the right person" we were sure that things would continue to be wonderful.

After having experienced two relationships that didn't work, I was convinced that I had just picked the *wrong* person in the past. Because Carlin was clearly the *right* person, I was sure things would be all downhill from here. I was sure we might have a few ups and downs, but I was looking for a "happily ever after" time of life.

We were both mature adults. We had each been married twice before and had children from our previous marriages. We knew what we wanted in a mate and had made out a detailed list. We had good jobs and shared interests. We were sure that the problems from our past were behind us and the future looked brilliantly exciting.

Oh, how naïve we were. It turned out that finding the right partner was just the first step and actually the easiest step. I believe there are five stages to a good marriage. I think of them in similar ways to the *Hero's Journey* described by Joseph Campbell. We don't often think of creating a marriage as a hero's journey, but anyone who has tried it knows that it is the most demanding, life-changing, and satisfying a journey that one can engage in their lives. Not everyone makes it successfully, but with good guidance, including a good "love map," most people can find real, lasting love.

Some people start the journey when they are young, but I don't believe anyone can complete the journey until they are fifty or older. I suspect it is a journey that will continue until we die, and perhaps even beyond that. Until we reach midlife we are still influenced by the marriage journey of our families, our friends, or our society. Once we've reached midlife we come to accept that this is our own journey. We can't let our parents, friends, or society dictate how to do the journey or even what kind of a journey it is.

The journey toward real, lasting love is unique to each person. We can be guided, but ultimately the path is ours alone. Joseph Campbell said this about the Hero's Journey: **"You enter the forest at the darkest point, where there is no path. Where there is a way or path, it is someone else's path. You are not on your own path. If you follow someone else's way, you are not going to realize your potential."**

Take a moment to read this again and let it sink in. What feelings does it bring up in you? Where are you on this path? Have you been following someone else's path? You might want to take some time to reflect and write down your thoughts and feelings.

This is a difficult truth to grasp. Often we think we're blazing our own trail, only to find out we are walking the path our mother or father walked. Sometimes we think we're living our relationship life our own way, but we're really rebelling against what our parents did or society dictates. Doing the *opposite* of what our parents did may seem like independence, but it's just another form of looking for love in all the wrong places.

Why Is This Important? Currently, our culture focuses a great deal of attention on finding the right partner. There are hundreds of websites that will help you find Mr. or Ms. *Right.* But there's much less focus on our internal love map. If our map is wrong, we're not likely to find the right person. Further, as difficult as it is to find a good mate, that turns out to be the easy part. Much more difficult is to make a good marriage that lasts and enhances the well-being of the couple.

Sharing the five stages of marriage and some of what I have learned will help you find your own, unique, path to joy. Here are the stages:

Stage 1: Falling in Love

Stage 2: Becoming a Couple

Stage 3: Disillusionment

Stage 4: Creating Real, Lasting Love

Stage 5: Finding Your Calling as a Couple

Step 1: Understand nature's purpose in having us fall in love in stage 1.

Here's a thought experiment that can teach us a lot. Imagine the implication of this simple truth: None of your direct ancestors died childless. We know your parents had at least one child. We also know your grandparents had at least one child. You can trace your ancestry back and back and back. You may or may not have children and you certainly know people who will never have children. But all your ancestors did.

How did they do that? Well, they *fell in love* or at least they *fell in lust*, which often accompanies falling in love. I call it nature's trick because it gets us together. It feels so good because all those hormones are triggered: testosterone, estrogen, dopamine, and many others. Without them we'd never make babies or stay together long enough for the babies to survive. Our species would disappear. Evolution and natural selection ensure that our species will have the best chance to survive. It starts with the wonderful-crazy feeling of falling in love.

Falling in love also feels so great because we project all our hopes and dreams on our lover. We imagine that they will fulfill our desires, give us all the things we didn't get as children, deliver on all the promises our earlier relationships failed to fulfill. We are sure we will remain *in love* forever. And because we are besotted with "love hormones," we're not aware of any of this.

Many of us look back on this period of romantic love and believe that this was the best time of our marriage. We remember the heat, the passion, the excitement, the wonder, the absolute clarity of a future filled with light and love. We laughed at curmudgeons like George Bernard Shaw who offered a darker vision of this stage of love:

When two people are under the influence of the most violent, most insane, most delusive, and most transient of passions, they are required to swear that they will remain in that excited, abnormal, and exhausting condition continuously until death do them part.

Helen Fisher, PhD, is a world-renowned scientist who has researched the reasons we fall in love and why we fall in love with that special person. She is a biological anthropologist, a senior research fellow at The Kinsey Institute, and chief scientific advisor to the Internet dating site Match.com. She says that falling in love is much more than a feeling. "Romantic love," she says, "is a mammalian brain system for mate choice." It's nature's trick to get us paired up. It involves two brain/hormonal systems: "lust" and "attraction."[1]

Lust is a strong desire to have sexual intercourse and is driven, in both men and women, by the hormones testosterone and estrogen. When we are attracted we lock into that special person and are truly love-struck and can think of little else. Scientists think that three main neurotransmitters are involved in this stage: adrenaline, dopamine, and serotonin.

The initial stages of falling in love activates our stress response, increasing our blood levels of adrenalin and cortisol. This is what causes our heart to race, our mouth to go dry, and we sweat when we are in the presence of our loved one. When Fisher scanned the brains of the "love-struck" couples she found high levels of the neurotransmitter dopamine. This chemical stimulates "desire and reward" by triggering intense rushes of pleasure. It has a similar effect to taking cocaine. Serotonin is responsible for the lovely preoccupation and focus we have on our partner.

But here's something few people know: Although that wonderful feeling of "falling in love" doesn't go on continually forever, it does not fade away, never to return. Dr. Fisher told me, **"Romantic love is like a sleeping cat. It can be re-awakened at any time."** It may get lost, but it can return again in stage 4. That's certainly what Carlin and I found.

Why Is This Important? It's understandable that we all have strongly positive memories of this stage of our relationship. But too many of us want to stay in this phase and feel we've lost something when the hormonally driven feelings of lust and attraction begin to wane. Further, as we hit stage 3, "Disillusionment," many couples break apart and feel there is something wrong with their marriage. "I love you, but I'm not *in love* with you anymore" becomes a constant refrain. As a result, too many men and women leave the relationship before reaching stages 4 and 5.

Whether we're planning to have children or not, nature connects us so that children who come into the world will have the love and protection of two parents. Throughout our evolutionary history children whose parents stayed together had the best chance of growing up and surviving long enough to have children of their own and keep our species going.

Step 2: Learn to bond with our partner in stage 2.

This is the stage where the power of two becomes apparent. This is a time when we may have children and raise them. If we don't have children, it's the time when our couple bond deepens and develops. It's a time of togetherness and joy. We learn what the other person likes, and we expand our individual lives to begin developing a life of "the two of us."

Once again our hormonal and brain function work together to enable us to connect more deeply with each other. Oxytocin, also known as "the cuddle hormone" and "the moral molecule," deepens the feeling of attachment and contributes to that loving feeling that we desire so strongly. Oxytocin is released by men and women during orgasm and also when they snuggle, touch, and look deeply into each other's eyes. The original purpose of oxytocin was likely to bond the mother to the baby, but like all hormones it has multiple effects in the body. The same loving feeling that bonds a mother (and father) to their infant baby girl or boy is present when we bond to our mate.

Another, related hormone, vasopressin, also contributes to the attachment and bonding process. The power of this important hormone was recognized by biologists studying a small rodent called a vole. Prairie voles engage in far more sex than is strictly necessary for reproductive purposes. Like humans, they also form fairly stable pair-bonds. However, when male prairie voles were given a drug that blocks the effect of vasopressin, the bond with their partner deteriorated, and they lost their devotion to their partner and failed to protect their partner from new suitors.

Why Is This Important? During this phase we experience less of the falling head-over-heels "in love" feelings. There is more of the feeling of deep affection and love for our partner. We feel warm and cuddly. The sex may not be as wild, but it's deeply bonding. We feel safe, cared for, cherished, and appreciated. We feel close and protected. We often think this is the ultimate level of love, and we expect it to go on forever. We are often blind-sided by the turnaround of stage 3.

Step 3: Recognize that disillusionment helps us get down to the real work of love and marriage in stage 3.

No one told us about stage 3 in understanding love and marriage. Stage 3 is where my first two marriages collapsed, and for too many relationships this is the beginning of the end. We all recognize stage 1 when we fall in love, and most of us are familiar with stage 2 where we start a family or settle into a warm, loving, committed relationship. In my first two marriages I thought this was all there was. I spent a lot of time looking for the right partner. When I found her I enjoyed months and years on a roller coaster high of fun and good times with my dream lover as we enjoyed the romantic, falling-in-love phase. We then spent many more years starting a family, making a living, and raising children.

But little by little things changed. We made love less often, but justified it because we were stressed trying to make a living while taking care of small children. We became more irritable with each other. We fought more, and the fights lasted longer and never fully resolved. Even when things seemed fine and we were back to feeling "in love" with each other, there were lingering hurts and misunderstandings that never went away and ate at the foundation of our relationship. I began to feel I could never do anything right, that nothing I did pleased her. She accused me of being withdrawn and moody. But there were still good things about our lives, and we both immersed ourselves in our work and family.

When we approached our tenth anniversary we couldn't ignore the fact that we were deeply unhappy. What had happened to our lives? What had happened to us? There was still love, but increasingly there was a feeling of something bordering on hate. There were times I felt I was the last person in the world she wanted to be around. We spent more time with our friends and busied ourselves in our work. The more disconnected we became from each other, the more we sought to get our needs met outside the relationship.

We finally sought out counseling. By then there was a mountain of hurts, resentments, and misunderstandings. Marriage and family counselors then, and to some degree now, still had the belief that when things are truly bad for the couple, it's better to go your separate ways. There is still a strong influence of independence in our society, and we are taught early the importance of being ourselves and doing our thing.

My first wife and I soon separated and then divorced. We felt we had done our best to make it work and our therapist felt the same. We always thought that we'd be kind to each other, even through a divorce, but our anger and pain blinded us to our underlying goodness and we fought over custody issues and later fought about just about anything. I still feel deep sadness for the pain I caused her and the children, and more pain was still to come.

Three years after our divorce I met and married a woman on the rebound, thinking all would be well. We had great highs and huge lows. She had a son who was living with her ex-husband and my children were living with my ex-wife. But visits together proved stressful and we stayed together only a few years.

Before I met Carlin, the woman I've been with now for thirty-six years, I decided I better learn more about love and marriage. I had definitely learned that being a marriage and family counselor didn't prevent me from having my own problems, and in fact may have contributed to some of my blind spots about marriage. The core of what I learned is contained in this book. The key things I learned were about what happens in stages 3, 4, and 5.

Why Is This Important? Most of us accept the reality that a marriage will have its ups and downs, but few of us understand that there is an actual stage in marriage where we will feel disconnected and estranged from each other, where we will feel we're living with a stranger and wonder who stole the loving partner we thought we had married. Because we're not aware of this stage or the stage beyond it, we believe that these bad times must mean that the marriage is not working. Too many people give up at this stage. They either leave the marriage or come to believe that this is the best they can hope for and accept a marriage of convenience rather than one of passion, joy, and continual growth.

Step 4: Appreciate the benefits of disillusionment.

Carlin and I went through the wonderful times of falling in love, merging our families, and building a life together. But when we started to have problems and became disillusioned, we were more prepared to deal with it. I'll describe our journey in more detail in the next chapter, but here I'll introduce you to a concept that saved us a great deal of grief and can help your relationship to get through this difficult phase.

When we fall in love, we are blinded to some important realities about ourselves and our partner. We project all our hopes and dreams on to them and think we see the partner that will meet all our needs, and erase the pain and disappointment about what we didn't get in our families growing up and what we didn't find in our previous relationships.

Disillusionment can mean that we feel we've made a mistake in who we picked as our partner. We may think about rectifying our error by finding a new partner in an attempt to distance ourselves and move on. It can also mean that we let go of our illusions and go deeper into the reality of what it truly means to love another person. When Carlin and I hit stage 3 after we were together for ten years, we hung in there and went deeper. Here are some of the illusions we became aware of and had to release:

— If there is conflict between us, someone must be to blame.
— A good marriage means that our love is constant and unwavering.
— If you really loved me you would_____. We each had our own set of fill-in-the-blanks.
— You would never have fantasies of being with another.
— You would always know what I need.
— You would always be kind and gentle.
— You would never be so wrapped up with yourself you wouldn't have time for me.
— If we're unhappy for more than a certain amount of time (e.g., a month, a year, three years) there must be something wrong with the marriage.

I can tell you that stage 3 is the most difficult period of time that anyone can experience. That's why most couples who hit this stage want to go back to the way it used to be. We lament that "You love me, but you're not *in love* with me." We are hungry for the romance we used to share and for the closeness and comfort that used to be so central to our relationship. We feel like we're in hell and we want out. It helped us to remember this bit of wisdom attributed to Winston Churchill: **"If you're going through hell, keep going."**

I found the advice helpful. When things are really bad in our relationship it can feel like hell. After months and years of being burned, we want out. As most of us are unaware there are four stages, it's not surprising that we try and go back to what we had or we bail out altogether. But I learned that the best is yet to come.

For most of my life I bought into the idea that love had only two stages. We fall in love, then love deepens and we live happily ever after. No one told me that we fall in love, love deepens, then we go through hell before love returns again. But that has been our experience.

It took us a long time to realize that the feelings of stress and conflict did not mean we had chosen the wrong person but, in fact, meant we had chosen just the right person with whom we could deepen our experience of love.

As a young couple, I still remember my first wife and I going to hear the legendary psychologist and therapist Carl Rogers talk about marriage. He was in his eighties then, and he and his wife had been married more than sixty years. My wife and I had been together for less than a year and were anxious to hear the great man's wisdom about love and life.

At one point in his talk he turned to his wife, Helen. "Remember that stretch when things were so bad in our relationship?" She smiled and nodded her head. I was amazed to hear that my idol had problems in his relationship. But I was dumbfounded to hear what came next. "There was that bad patch of nine or ten years when things were awful." Helen smiled and shook her head as she too remembered. "But we hung in there and worked things out."

"You must be kidding," I thought. "Nine or ten years of things being awful?" I couldn't imagine things ever being awful for me and my wife, and if they ever were I sure couldn't imagine staying in a *state of awful* for nine or ten years.

Now having been married for thirty-six years, I understand that there can be some pretty terrible times. But getting through those times together is how we learn about real, lasting love. The key to getting on the road to real, lasting love is to understand the purpose of stages 3 and 4.

I suspect that we wouldn't need stage 3 and 4 if all of us were raised in families that were totally loving and supportive, and we lived in a world where all families' needs for safety, security, and love were supported 100 percent. But that is not the case. All of us suffer from some degree of childhood neglect and abuse. Even if we had parents who had no problems of their own and were totally tuned in to our needs as a child, there would still be some degree of trauma.

What happens in stage 3 is that our initial desires for love, that we thought we'd have met in stages 1 and 2, run up against the realities that we had projected our ideals on a real-life person. The degree of conflict we feel in stage 3 is the inevitable result of the clash between our dreamed-for lover who was going to heal all our old wounds and the reality of a real-life person with wounds of their own.

Step 5: Accept that the purpose of stage 3 is to uncover the wounds from previous relationships.

After many years of living and learning I found out that the hidden purpose of stage 3 is to uncover the wounds we experienced in childhood and to surface them so that they can be healed. We might amend our marriage vows to include something along these lines: "Not only will I stay with you in sickness and in health, but I will be with you when our collective wounds from childhood and our previous relationships cause us to panic and hunger for healing at the same time we deny our need for healing."

When I looked at my own conflicts and those of my clients I realized that most all of them were related to wounds that occurred first in childhood and were perpetuated in later relationships. You'll learn more about how to recognize and address these wounds in the next chapter.

Step 6: Recognize that healing each other's wounds is the great gift of stage 4.

We can't really have real, lasting love as long as we have unhealed relationship wounds. Once we recognize that the purpose of stage 3 is to surface the old wounds so that we can deal with them in the context of an adult, loving relationship, we can understand that the core of real, lasting love is to be partners in healing these wounds. This is the great gift of stage 4, to heal our wounds together.

We can't heal by ourselves. We can only heal partnership wounds in a partnership that allows each partner to go more deeply into their lives and to be vulnerable enough with their partner that the deep healing of relationship can be activated.

Why Is This Important? Once we understand that the turmoil in stage 3 doesn't mean there's something wrong with the marriage, we can relax a bit. It still can feel hellish at times, but so, too, can going to the dentist. But if we know it's part of the healing process we can get through it more easily. Because most of us have a series of wounds from the past and illusions that must be recognized and processed, we will likely go through stage 3 multiple times, which will deepen and expand the love we can give and receive at stage 4. When we understand the purpose of stage 3 and stage 4, we can bring all the necessary tools together to make this difficult, yet rewarding, journey the best it can be.

Step 7: Find your calling as a couple in stage 5.

When we get to midlife and beyond, we all have a desire to make a difference in the world. We usually think of this as our "calling" in life. At a time when we must face the reality that we must change our lives to live sustainably on the planet, many of us feel called upon to address these issues. My calling has been to help men and women find real, lasting love so that together we can save humanity. My calling goes beyond my own personal joy in creating my relationship with Carlin. I want to make a difference in the world. This is true of Carlin as well.

The Power of Two enables us to do together what we could never do alone. My calling puts me more in the public arena worldwide, but I couldn't do it without Carlin's backing and support. Her calling is to make a difference with our family, friends, and community. I'm there for her, and my support allows her to make her own difference in the world.

You might ask yourselves what you see as your calling in life. What do you feel called upon to do, that would make the world a little better place? I believe that two people who are experiencing real, lasting love can commit themselves to sharing that love with the world. Think what the world would be like if more and more of us were engaged in expressing real, lasting love.

In the next chapter we'll take a look at the ways in which being part of a couple can empower your life. You'll get a chance to make a renewed commitment to the love you want to have. You'll begin to reflect on your own situation and learn about how our complex and magical brain can make love wonderful, but also confusing.

Two

The Power of Two: Make a Commitment to Love

*A*ll of us have busy lives. In a topsy-turvy economy and a world that seems stressed to the max, we've got a lot to do just keeping ourselves afloat. We don't have an endless amount of time and energy to focus on keeping our relationship alive and well or finding a new relationship if we're starting all over again. I want to help you cut through the forest of confusion and get you on the right track.

Step 1: Make an honest assessment of your commitment to love.

There's an old story about the guy holding a pencil. His wife asks him to toss it to her. He gestures to toss it, but the pencil doesn't leave his hand. She says again, "Toss it to me." Once again he gestures, but the pencil traces an arc, but never leaves his hand. She asks a third time and he repeats the move, saying, "I'm trying." The moral, in the words of the great philosopher, Yoda, from *Star Wars,* "Do, or do not . . . There is no try."

So, make an honest assessment of your commitment to having real, lasting love. On a scale of 1 to 10, ask yourself "How much do I want to have real, lasting love in my life?" A rating of 1 is very little, and 10 is absolutely the very highest desire. Write down the number you have chosen.

Desire is only one part of commitment. The other part is hope for success. Again, on a scale of 1 to 10, ask yourself "How confident am I that I can have real, lasting love in my life?" A rating of 1 is very little confidence, and 10 is absolute confidence in your ability to have it.

Most people who are serious about having real, lasting love give themselves a score of 8 or higher on the "I want" scale. But they may give themselves a much lower rating on the "can have" scale.

That's not surprising because we seem to experience so many more failures than successes. I'll show you the reasons for that as we move ahead. You'll find your "can have" assessment will improve. For now, if your desire is high we can move ahead to the next step.

Step 2: Put your faith in the Power of Two.

We live at a time when we celebrate the power of the individual. We focus on sports heroes like Ted Williams, Magic Johnson, Michael Jordan, and Joe Montana. We marvel at the success of business tycoons like Steve Jobs, Bill Gates, and Warren Buffet. We idolize movie stars like George Clooney, Meryl Streep, Kate Winslet, and Robert De Niro.

In the field of psychology, "self-actualization" is seen as the ultimate goal that men and women aspire to achieve. Successful entrepreneurs are the darlings of business, and we live at a time when personal happiness seems more important than the well-being of the group.

In our most intimate relationships we want to connect and bond, but we also want to be free to find our own happiness. I've found that this bias toward the individual causes many people to give up too soon when a relationship is in trouble. Sometimes one person is committed to making things better while the other person feels hopeless and wants to leave.

Sixteenth-century English poet and cleric John Donne recognized that there is something larger than the individual in these immortal words: "No man is an island, entire of itself; every man is a piece of the continent, a part of the main." Although poetic, Donne misses the importance of the dyad. We are each conceived from a man and a woman. We were raised by a couple (or we wish we had been), and we all seek the love of that special someone.

Joshua Wolf Shenk maintains in his monumental book, *Powers of Two: How Relationships Drive Creativity*, that "two" has a power that few of us have fully recognized. He begins the book with a quote from Pulitzer Prize–winning playwright Tony Kushner, who maintains, **"The smallest indivisible human unit is two people, not one, one is a fiction."**[1] Take a moment to let that sink in. The idea that one is a fiction, and two is the basic unit, taps something deep in our collective souls.

When my wife, Carlin, and I got married she told me she was committed to the relationship. At the time I didn't fully understand the importance of what she was saying. Both of us had been married previously. We had made the traditional vows to love, honor, and cherish our partner "until death do you part." In our previous relationships, we had not stayed together throughout our lives and when things become difficult and it didn't seem that our needs were being met, we reverted to a focus on "me" rather than "we."

Carlin had a larger vision. She recognized that committing to the partnership rather than to the other or to ourselves would create a stronger bond and ultimately would serve us as individuals and as a family. "Thirty-six years later, I'm still learning to appreciate the wisdom of her vision and the creative Power of Two. What would your relationship be like if you committed to the relationship?" Take a moment to think about it. You might want to write down your thoughts and feelings.

Why Is This Important? If you're the one hanging in there, don't give up. If you are the one who has given up, I want you to know you can have the joy you feel you have lost. For both members of the couple I want you to know you can be close, yet free. The best is yet to be. If you're presently single, but wanting real, lasting love, don't give up. You can find the right person and learn to make the relationship work for both of you.

Step 3: Recognize "you two" and the power of intimate separateness.

In my first marriage I remember what I came to call "the approach–avoidance dance." My first wife and I would feel very close and connected. Then one of us would start a fight or some other friction would pull us apart and we'd become more distant. I thought it was because we were afraid of intimacy.

Since Carlin and I have been together, I've come to see that real, lasting love involves both intimacy and separation. The Power of Two reminds us that we have to learn to be close. But there's an equally valuable need to be separate. Focusing on "you two" reminds us that we need both. "Two" reminds us that we are part of a dyad; at the most basic level, we all come from the merging of two, a man and a woman. "You" reminds us that just as a child must separate from their parents in order to become a fully formed adult, so too must each of us have a life separate from the other.

If we have too much togetherness, love suffers. If we have too much separateness, love suffers. I remember someone telling me that "life is a dance we each do separately, together." My colleague Michael Gurian captures this dynamic in his book, *Lessons of Lifelong Intimacy.* Gurian says, "Intimate separateness is the daily balance of two equally necessary components of natural human attachment, intimacy and separateness. If either is neglected, love will fail."[2]

Further, two of the components for love are passion and eroticism. Where intimacy helps foster emotional connection, separation is necessary for a full expression of sexual passion. In her book *Mating in Captivity: Reconciling the Erotic and the Domestic,* couples and family therapist Esther Perel says, "In the course of establishing security, many couples confuse love with merging. This mix-up is a bad omen for sex. **To sustain an élan toward the other, there must be a synapse to cross. Eroticism requires separateness."**[3]

Though we live in a culture that prizes the individual, we focus our attention on overcoming our separateness by achieving greater intimacy with a partner. "Our culture tends to focus almost exclusively on closeness (what we tend to call 'intimacy' and 'romance,' says Gurian), "so much so that millions of couples lack the balance of closeness and *psychological separateness* necessary for long-lasting love."

Perhaps no one captured this dance of intimate separateness better than the poet Kahlil Gibran. In *The Prophet,* he offers this wisdom that all who wish for real, lasting love must heed:

> Let there be spaces in your togetherness, And let the winds of the heavens dance between you. Love one another but make not a bond of love: Let it rather be a moving sea between the shores of your souls. Fill each other's cup but drink not from one cup. Give one another of your bread but eat not from the same loaf. Sing and dance together and be joyous, but let each one of you be alone. Even as the strings of a lute are alone though they quiver with the same music. Give your hearts, but not into each other's

keeping. For only the hand of Life can contain your hearts. And stand together, yet not too near together: For the pillars of the temple stand apart, And the oak tree and the cypress grow not in each other's shadow.[4]

When I was younger I thought real love involved getting closer and closer until we were one. But now I see love more like the ocean waves washing to shore and then retreat in the opposite direction. I've seen that love dies when two people become distant and estranged from each other. But it dies equally often when two people become overly enmeshed and neglect the creative separation and aloneness that enable our separate souls to grow and flourish.

Where are you on the continuum of intimacy–separation? Do you find you are too close or do you feel you are too distant? Ask your partner how they feel. Finding the balance is a dynamic process. It changes over time and, like life, we must continually adjust as our needs change.

Why Is This Important? Too often couples conflict around how much intimacy and separation are needed. We can feel that our partner doesn't love us if they're wanting more distance than is comfortable for us. It's important to remember that there isn't any "right" balance. We each need to find it in our relationship, and it often changes over time. We must continually hear our partner and recalibrate as necessary.

Step 4: Renew your relationship with your partner at least every fifteen years.

Many of us made a vow when we married to remain committed to our partner until "death do we part." Whether we used those words, we still believe that once we make a commitment to our beloved, we will stay together for the long haul. What we fail to recognize is that for most of human history, the "long haul" was relatively short. As recently as the beginning of the twentieth century the life expectancy for men and women in the United States was less than fifty years.

Now, our life expectancy may be eighty, ninety, or one hundred years. The world is changing faster and faster, and so are our expectations and needs in our relationship. We're not the same people we were when we said, "I do." If we don't recognize the changes that go on in our relationship and adjust accordingly, it is easy to begin moving in different directions and for the relationship to come apart.

My wife, Carlin, and I had been married twice before when we met and fell in love. When we said, "I do" we wanted it to last. We didn't want to have another break-up and to have to start all over again. But we also recognized that we would change over time. We first got married on the island of St. Thomas in the Virgin Islands (seemed like a playfully ironic place to wed for the third time).

After fifteen years we came back to the Virgin Islands as part of a retreat with anthropologist Angeles Arrien and Native American elder Brooke Medicine Eagle. We had known Angie and Brooke for many years and asked if we could create a remarriage ceremony, which they agreed to help facilitate. I still have pictures of Angie covered in a veil chanting from her Basque tradition and Brooke smiling on while Carlin and I recited our new vows.

Fifteen years later we again reflected on our life and renewed our vows in Prague, where our son, Aaron, and his wife, Helena, are living. It turned out to be on the anniversary of Helena's parents, and we celebrated with them after we had our own ceremony at an old castle restaurant outside of Prague.

Thinking about our lives in the previous fifteen years, how we'd changed, what was important to us, what our commitment to the relationship looked like at this time, and what we wanted for the future gave us a chance to deepen our connection and update our love. I recommend that everyone have re-marriage ceremonies at suitable intervals. Real, lasting love is only as strong as the partnership, and the partnership changes through time and needs to be constantly updated.

What were the vows you made when you first married? What vows are still alive for you now? What changes have occurred in your lives that make it clear an update is necessary? What new vows would you like to make? Who would you like to be with you to share your recommitment to love?

Step 5: Accept our multiple-personality, four-part mammalian brain.

There's already too much negativity in the world, and I don't want to add to it. We often use animal terms to denigrate men and women. We say women are catty and men are dirty dogs. Growing up I was called a shrimp because I was short. But I think it's very helpful to understanding who we are if we recognize how our brains have evolved.

One of the important things to know about evolution, which we often forget, is that animals, including humans, aren't designed from scratch. New adaptations are added on to old ones. This is true of our brains. In his wonderfully creative book (including one of the best titles I've ever read), *Thank God for Evolution*, Michael Dowd draws on current brain science to describe the four brains that we all have and their evolutionary origins.

Our Reptilian Brain: Lizard Legacy

The cerebellum and the brain stem are the most primitive parts of our brain. These structures are represented by the lizard. But reptiles also include crocodiles, alligators, snakes, and turtles.

When I get really mad and upset, my wife says I get a beady-eyed look like a snake. I often accuse her of snapping my head off or disappearing into her shell like some ancient turtle.

"Our ancient reptilian brain is the seat of instinctual drives that are least subject to conscious control," says Dowd. "I call these primordial drives, 'the 3 S's of our inherited proclivities. They are *safety, sustenance,* and *sex.*"[5]

Think of the problems we have when we feel threatened or unsafe. We often fight, flee, or freeze. The problems Carlin has with me are often about her fears when I become angry (fight). I have problems when Carlin withdraws (flight) or closes down, and I feel shut out (freeze). We tell ourselves we should eat healthy food, but end up with a carton of late-night ice cream, hence our bulging waistlines. Our proclivity for sex doesn't always jibe with our conscious commitments and doing what is right. Men and women may cheat on each other, watch porn on the Internet, and have a secret sex life.

Our reptilian brain isn't very social (no one tries to cuddle up with a lizard). It wants what it wants, when it wants it, and isn't greatly concerned about the needs of others. The reptilian brain's mantra is "Me, Me, Me," which isn't a bad mantra. Reptiles have been on the planet for 200 million years, and our own reptile brain keeps us alive. But, we also have three other parts of our brains. As Michael Dowd would say, "Thank God for evolution."[6]

Old Mammalian Brain: The Furry Li'l Mammal

The limbic brain came into being with the first mammals. Reptiles don't have these brain structures. This part of the brain allows us to record memories of what is agreeable and disagreeable. It does this through our emotions. Simply stated, "If it feels good, do it, but if it feels bad, avoid it." The primary structures of the limbic brain are the hippocampus, the amygdala, and the hypothalamus. The limbic brain is the seat of the value judgments that we make, often subconsciously, that exert such a strong influence on our behavior.

This is also the center for nurturing the young and also for the bonds of love and affiliation that are present in adults. Problems often arise in relationships because these parts of our brain operate subconsciously. With Carlin, I may not be aware of when she needs to be held or appreciated. We often hunger for love, but we miss the cues from the other that would tell us how to respond.

New Mammalian Brain: Monkey Mind

"The part of the brain, the neocortex," says Dowd, "could be called our chatterbox, calculator, or computer brain because it is incessantly talking to itself (fretting about the past and worrying about the future), performing rudimentary cost-benefit analyses, and computing the balance of favors and debts in each of Furry Li'l Mammals social relationships."[7]

We all know this part of the brain when we are awake at night worrying about paying the bills or about the health and well-being of our kids. We also know it when we find ourselves ruminating over old grievances. This drives me nuts when I feel like Carlin isn't paying enough attention to me or I'm giving too much and not getting enough in return.

Prefrontal Cortex: Higher Porpoise

Our frontal lobes, the part of the brain just behind our eyes, is the most recently evolved. Elkhonon Goldberg, PhD, is clinical professor of neurology at New York University School of Medicine and author of numerous books on the brain. In his book *The Executive Brain: Frontal Lobes and the Civilized Mind*, he says, "The frontal lobes perform the most advanced and complex functions

in all the brain, the so-called executive functions. They are linked
to intentionality, purposefulness, and complex decision making.
**They reach significant development only in humans; arguably,
they make us human."**[8]

This is the part of the brain that can orchestrate all the other
parts. It can free the lizard in us to go after what we want and
protect our lives. It can also engage us to bond with our children,
love our mate, worry about the future, and live our full potential
in connected pairs. "It is here that we can create and nurture a
higher purpose," says Dowd, "which I delight in calling "higher
porpoise."[9]

I can't tell you how many couples I've seen (and I've certainly
experienced this in my own marriages) who tell me their partner
has changed. "He/She used to be so loving, caring, and attentive.
I could trust and count on them. Now he/she has become someone I don't even know."

Most of us want to think of our partner as always operating from their higher porpoise. When we fall in love and get
married, that's the person we think we're marrying. We're set
up for disappointment if we don't recognize that there is also a
chattering Monkey in us, a Furry Li'l Mammal, and a Snake or
Snapping Turtle.

Why Is This Important? Too often we neglect to take into account
that we are part of the animal kingdom. We often think of ourselves as apart from other animals and are then surprised when
we act in ways that seem out of character. If we can honor all parts
of ourselves and our partner, we will be more understanding when
we act in ways that may seem to be "immature" or "hurtful."

Step 6: Embrace love; let go of fear.

John Gottman, PhD, is one of the world's leading experts on marriage and family. In his famous "love lab" he has developed a

scientifically sound body of information that can accurately predict which marriages will do well and which ones will fall apart. In his book *What Makes Love Last? How to Build Trust and Avoid Betrayal* he offers a simple, yet profound understanding that can help us all improve our relationship lives.

In working with thousands of couples over a period of more than forty years he found that there is a single toxin that undermines people's commitment to each other. "It is a noxious invader, arriving with great stealth, undermining a seemingly stable romance until it may be too late," he says. **"The name of this toxin is *betrayal*."**[10] When most of us think of betrayal, we think of a sexual affair. And certainly infidelity is one of the most obvious and painful forms of betrayal.

But betrayals are often much more subtle and can go unrecognized by the couple until the structure of the marriage collapses under the weight of pain and confusion. Often one or both partners wonder "What the hell happened? How did it come to this?" Betrayal is a silent killer that masquerades as "the ups and downs of everyday life." Most couples are not even aware that they are betraying their partner or that they are suffering from their partner's betrayal.

This came home to me and my wife when we looked more deeply at how we often handled conflict. I would feel hurt and misunderstood and would become irritable and angry. Sometimes I would yell. Other times I would just go silent. Carlin would say, "You get that beady-eyed look that is frightening." To protect herself she would often close up emotionally and withdraw her affection. Even when I tried to make up, she would remain closed like a clam and I felt lost and alone.

It never occurred to either of us that my anger was a kind of betrayal because it undermined her sense of safety and she lost trust in me. Likewise, her emotional withdrawal caused me to feel that I couldn't make a mistake without being punished by her closing down her affections. Betrayals are common, and they are so prevalent in relationships we often don't recognize them. Here some common betrayals I've witnessed in my own life and in the thousands of couples I have treated:

— If one partner puts their career ahead of their relationship, that is a betrayal.
— If one partner puts the needs of the children ahead of the relationship, that is betrayal.
— If one partner acts in ways that frighten the other, that is betrayal.
— If one partner is critical, judgmental, and blaming, that is betrayal.
— If one partner withdraws their affection, that is betrayal.
— If one partner lies to the other, that is betrayal.

Not only is betrayal universal (remember we all are snakes and snapping turtles out to protect ourselves and get what we want when we want it), but we often betray our partner without being aware of it and with the best of intentions. We work long hours away from home in an attempt to love and support our family. We cancel our date night because the kids seem to need us more. We become angry when we feel threatened and we withdraw to protect ourselves.

When we get to the heart of why we betray our partners in small and large ways, it boils down to fear. We're afraid of losing something that is precious to us. We're afraid we won't have enough money. We're afraid something will happen to our kids. We're afraid we will lose respect. We're afraid we'll be alone. We're afraid we'll die if we don't get (fill in the blank: sex, love, sweets, etc.) when and where we want them.

Learning to recognize and minimize these common betrayals can go a long way toward healing the wounds that pull us apart.

Trust is the glue that holds us together and provides the safety and security for love to flourish. We may imagine that what is pulling us apart are things like boredom, lack of mutual interests, unhappiness, falling out of love, value conflicts, drinking problems, sexual dysfunction, or just growing apart. But these are all the result of a long series of betrayals that build up over time.

Love can heal all wounds. According to Jerry Jampolsky, MD, author of the classic *Love Is Letting Go of Fear*, "The world we see that seems so insane is the result of a belief system that is not working. To perceive the world differently, we must be willing to change our belief system, let the past slip away, expand our sense of now, and dissolve the fear in our minds."[11]

Carlin and I lived in Marin County and met Dr. Jampolsky soon after he founded the Center for Attitudinal Healing. Carlin worked at the center during those early years. Here are some of the ideas from *Love Is Letting Go of Fear* that we can put into practice in our lives, particularly our love lives:

- Peace of mind comes from not wanting to change others.
- You can be right or you can be happy.
- The first fifty years Jampolsky believed there was a pot of gold at the end of the rainbow, and it was his goal to find that pot of gold. Now be believes that we are the rainbow, the pot of gold is love, and that is who we actually are.
- Our brain can flip from love to fear and back to love in the blink of an eye, much like those optical illusions where we first see a beautiful woman or an old hag, a chalice or two figures facing each other.

Why Is This Important? In order to have real, lasting love, we have to work to know ourselves and our partner. That isn't easy. With the constant demands of our world to make a living, take care of family, deal with health issues, and worry about the future we often don't take time to truly know ourselves and our partner. The good news about a crisis in the relationship is that we are forced to take the time. Fear is a potent motivator. It gets our attention and forces us to act. It reminds us to come back to a focus on love. The good news that I'll be reminding us again and again is that we can keep coming back to a focus on love, no matter how many times we fall into fear.

Fear alerts us to danger. But fear can also block our ability to love deeply and well. In the next chapter we'll look at the roots of our fears and how our early childhood experiences continue to influence our lives, for better or worse.

Three

Healing Childhood Trauma Can Save Your Marriage

*U*nderstanding the five stages of marriage helped me better understand why my first two marriages ended when we couldn't resolve the issues we faced in stage 3. We couldn't seem to get out of the negative spirals that pulled us down. I saw similar things happening with other couples and did my best to help them. I not only felt discouraged about my own love life, but I felt like a fraud trying to help others achieve success where I had failed.

I was sure there must be something I was missing that kept me, and so many others, from a long-term committed relationship with real, lasting love. The answer I found surprised me. An increasing body of research and clinical practice pointed to unresolved childhood trauma as the missing link. These unresolved childhood traumas were like time bombs quietly ticking away until they exploded again and again, often many years later, and would sink marriage after marriage.

You wouldn't know it from meeting him today, but Dr. James Doty, an extremely successful neurosurgeon, the director of the Center for Compassion and Altruism Research and Care

(CCARE) and a close, personal friend of the Dalai Lama, grew up in an extremely traumatic home environment. The family was very poor; his father was an angry, unreliable alcoholic; and his mother was chronically depressed and suicidal. In his book, *Into the Magic Shop: A Neurosurgeon's Quest to Discover the Mysteries of the Brain and the Secrets of the Heart,* he shares the four practices he learned as a boy that helped him heal the wounds from his childhood and become a successful physician, healer, and entrepreneur. Dr. Doty demonstrates that trauma can be healed, and we can all learn to live and love more fully.[1]

But without this deep healing, I've seen the majority of marriages fail, either ending in divorce and separation or devolving into bitterness and dysfunction. We know from years of research by marriage experts John and Julie Gottman that successful marriages share two traits: **kindness and generosity.** John Gottman began his research with couples in 1986, when he set up "The Love Lab" at the University of Washington.

With a team of researchers, they hooked the couples up to electrodes and asked the couples to speak about their relationship, like how they met, a major conflict they were facing together, and a positive memory they had. As they spoke, the electrodes measured the subjects' blood flow, heart rates, and how much sweat they produced. Then the researchers sent the couples home and followed up with them six years later to see if they were still together.

From the data they gathered, Gottman separated the couples into two major groups: the "masters" and "disasters" of relationships. The masters were still happily together after six years. The disasters had either broken up or were chronically unhappy in their marriages. In fact, in research over the last twenty years, the Gottmans have been able to predict with 94-percent accuracy which couples are likely to become masters of their relationship, able to be kind and generous, even under stress, and which relationships will end in disaster, with couples divorcing or living *unhappily ever after.*

What the Gottmans found in their "Love Lab" were two types of communication during day-to-day interaction. If the typical response is *ignoring, dismissive, minimizing,* or *attacking,* that couple will not likely last or be miserable if they remain together. If the typical response is *engaging, supportive, interested,* or *caring* that couple will survive and thrive. They found that closing off feelings and contempt are killers, while kindness and generosity of spirit nurture the relationship.[2]

So, the million-dollar question is "Why aren't couples kinder and more generous?" Why would we ignore or attack someone we loved? The Gottmans got clues when they analyzed the physiological reactions of the couple when they interacted. When the "master" couples interacted, their physiology was relaxed. They were easy with each other and their body reactions showed it. When the "disaster" couples interacted, their physiological reactions were in stress mode. They were on alert, reactive, easily triggered. Even when they were being nice to each other, they were ready for "fight or flight." Rather than feeling safe, they were on alert for danger, ready to defend and protect themselves at the slightest hint of a threat.

When I read this it rang true from my experience. Looking back at my failed relationships, I remember that feeling of disease with my partner. I could never shake the feeling that I was always walking on eggshells. I never knew when I might be criticized or blamed. Even when things were good between us, I never was able to totally relax.

Why Is This Important? If our brains keep us on hyper-alert when we're with our partner, we are always looking for danger. Every word, look, or movement can be misinterpreted as a threat. When we're under stress, as most of us are today, it's easy to get triggered. Because our partner is often as stressed as we are, it's not surprising that we each trigger a reaction in the other. Over time we begin seeing our partner as the enemy, rather than our loving friend. The question is "why?" and the answer turns out to be *how many aces we hold*. Let me explain.

The Adverse Childhood Experiences (ACE) Study is an ongoing collaboration between the Centers for Disease Control and Prevention in Atlanta and Kaiser Permanente in San Diego. It is one of the largest investigations ever conducted to assess associations between childhood maltreatment and later-life health and well-being.

The ACE Study has published more than 70 research papers since 1998, and hundreds of additional research papers based on the ACE Study have also been published. In addition, a recently published book, *Childhood Disrupted: How Your Biography Becomes Your Biology, and How You Can Heal* by Donna Jackson Nakazawa[3] offers the latest information that can assist us in healing ourselves and healing our relationships. A website, AcesTooHigh.com, offers updated information on ACE research and practice.

Here are a few of the important findings:

- ACEs are common. Sixty-four percent of adults have at least one.
- ACEs don't occur alone. If you have one, there's an 87-percent chance that you have two or more.
- The more ACEs you have, the greater the risk for relationship problems, chronic disease, violence and being a victim of violence, and mental health problems such as anxiety and depression.
- Childhood trauma and wounding are like a series of asteroid strikes that creates a fog of distress that interferes with our love map. We can't see where we are going or how to get the love we need.

— Even though childhood trauma is common and can have lasting effects on our relationships and our health, it's never too late to heal.

Step 1: Get your ACE score and learn what it means.

When I took the ACE test (which you can *do http://acestoohigh.com /got-your-ace-score/*), I found that I had four ACEs. That's a good thing to have if you're playing poker, but not so good for your personal and relationship health. Having an ACE score of 4 increases the risk of emphysema or chronic bronchitis by nearly 400 percent, and suicide by 1,200 percent. People with high ACE scores are more likely to be violent, and to have more marriages, more broken bones, more drug prescriptions, more depression, and more autoimmune diseases.

For the first time I made the connection between my father's attempted suicide when I was five, his absence from our home, my mother's constant anxiety and worry, and my adult depression, manic depressive illness (bipolar), breathing problems, and heart arrhythmias. ACEs were the missing links that helped me understand why my relationships started off well, but turned fearful and angry, and more importantly what I could do to heal the past so my relationship could survive and thrive.

Why Is This Important? Recognizing the importance of childhood trauma to the problems people have in their adult relationships was the key to unlocking the door that keeps so many people from achieving real, lasting love. These childhood wounds often get triggered in the third stage of marriage, "Disillusionment"; but without understanding how ACEs impact us, we often blame our partner, come to believe we've made the wrong choice, end the marriage, and try to start all over again with someone else. Understanding ACEs gives us the tools we need to move beyond stage 3 to the joys of real, lasting love.

Step 2: Recognize that other traumas can also impact our relationships.

I think of the ten ACE traumas as the "big asteroid" strikes that can impact our lives. But I've found that other traumas, which may seem less important, can also have a powerful effect on our adult lives. Multiple "small asteroid" strikes can cloud our vision. Here are ten that I've found to be important. Which ones have you experienced? What other wounds would you add to the list?

1. Were you sick when you were young?
2. Did your parent leave you alone, even for a short time, and you panicked?
3. Did you lose a close friend because they died, moved away, or went to another school?
4. Were you teased or bullied?
5. Were you rejected by a close friend or excluded from groups you wanted to join?
6. Did someone close to you betray your trust?
7. Did you feel different from your peers because of things like your height, weight, or other characteristics that made you stand out?
8. Did you go through physical change such as a handicap or injury or a growth spurt or other physical changes at puberty?
9. Were one or both parents withdrawn and distant or irritable and anxious?
10. Did you feel wounded or betrayed in a past love relationship?

When you look over the ten ACEs and the ten additions, they may trigger other memories of trauma that may resonate in your body in the same way as the ones you checked. Write those down here:

You may also want to keep a journal and detail some of these "hits" from the past and how they may be affecting your present relationships.

Why Is This Important? Most of us dismiss traumatic experiences. Whether we have a large number or a few, whatever we experience comes to feel "normal." As children, we need to believe in our parents' goodness for our survival. As a result, we deny these events, even to ourselves. When we allow ourselves to remember and say "Yes, this did happen to me," we begin to free ourselves from our traumatic past and can begin the path of healing ourselves and our relationships. Further, past wounds have a way of reverberating later in life and cause us to re-create situations that harmed us in the past. For instance, if felt abandoned as a child, we may expect abandonment later in life and actually help create the very thing we fear. But knowledge is power. The more we know, the more resilient we can become.

Step 3: Understand that the body keeps score.

It has taken me years to remember many of these early traumas and to understand their importance. Once we are open to remembering, we begin to get more information from our body, mind, and spirit. Even though our conscious mind may have blocked out trauma, our body knows.

Take a moment to review the traumatic experiences you checked from the ten from the ACE study and the additional ten listed above. You may want to close your eyes and ask your body to share its memories. You may feel coldness or heat in some parts of your body. You may feel an emptiness or you may notice your breathing speeds up. Trust that your body is trying to let you know that these experiences have impacted your life and your body is open to healing.

Bessel Van Der Kolk, MD, is one of the world's leading experts on trauma. In his book *The Body Keeps the Score: Brain, Mind, and Body in the Healing of Trauma,* he says, "Trauma affects not only those who are directly exposed to it, but also those around them. The wives of men who suffer from PTSD tend to become depressed, and the children of depressed mothers are at risk of growing up insecure and anxious. . . . Long after a traumatic experience is over, it may be reactivated at the slightest hint of danger and mobilize disturbed brain circuits and secrete massive amounts of stress hormones."[4]

Why Is This Important? I always wondered why there were certain things my wife did that seemed to trigger a reaction. She'd make a seemingly innocuous comment and I'd get angry. Or she'd be a little late coming home at night and I'd get anxious. It was like something was triggered inside my brain that would set me off. I finally understood that early traumatic experiences keep us on alert and present experiences, even small ones, can set up a resonance in our body that triggers the feelings from our past. This helped me not to blame my wife when something she said triggered me or to blame myself when something I said, or did, triggered her.

Step 4: Learn how childhood stress impacts our brain and has a lasting impact on our health.

When we moved to the country everything scared me—the bugs, the bears, the unknown. To learn to overcome my fears I decided to sleep out on our deck. I remember the first night: I had just fallen asleep and I heard a sound in the forest. I was immediately alert. My heart began to pound and I wondered if it was a bear, a mountain lion (yes, we have them where I live), or a prowler. I was attuned to the possible danger and my body prepared for "fight or flight."

A small area of the brain known as the hypothalamus released hormones that stimulated the pituitary and adrenal glands to pump out chemical messengers throughout my body. Adrenaline and cortisol triggered immune cells to secrete powerful molecules, including inflammatory cytokines, to stir up my body's immune response in case I had to fight.

But then I saw a little fawn walk by in the moonlight and I began to relax. My breathing slowed and my mind relaxed. My hypothalamus, pituitary, and adrenal glands (the HPA stress axis) brought everything back to normal and I drifted back to sleep.

This is the normal response to acute stress. We are put on alert, we deal with the danger, and our bodies return to their original relaxed state. But when we are subjected to trauma, as children, that is chronic and unpredictable, our whole system remains on alert. We never know when danger will strike so we are always revved up and ready to react. This leads to unregulated inflammation, which can cause all kinds of diseases later in life. For instance, I was diagnosed with an adrenal tumor when I was fifty. It didn't occur to me at the time that it was related to my early childhood traumas.

"When the HPA stress axis is overloaded in childhood or the teen years," says Donna Nakazawa, author of *Childhood Disrupted*, "it leads to long-lasting side effects—not just because of the impact stress has on us at that time in our lives, but also because early chronic stress biologically reprograms how we will react to stressful events for our entire lives."[5]

Why Is This Important? Many of us have a difficult time accepting that childhood trauma can still impact our health years later. When we understand that our stress systems never turn off and go back to normal, we can see why the past is never really in the past until we heal it. It's as though we're hooked up to an intravenous line dripping poisonous inflammatory chemicals into our veins year after year. We may become used these chemicals so we don't notice their effect. It's no wonder that these childhood traumas produce problems when we're thirty, forty, fifty, sixty, and beyond, including depression, heart disease, asthma, auto-immune disease, ulcers, chronic fatigue, cancer, and of course, broken relationships.

Step 5: Recognize the impact of chronic unpredictable toxic stress (CUTS).

The kinds of trauma we've been discussing are different from single-event trauma, such as a natural disaster where everyone knows about it and wants to help. These traumas occur behind closed doors and we are told to keep them secret. They can also go on for many years. Whether it is an uncle molesting a daughter or a mother becoming emotionally over-involved with a son, there is often a sense of shame that we keep buried inside. Although some trauma is like a huge explosion in our lives, such as my father's suicide attempt, others are more like a thousand cuts of pain that may seem minor, but can kill us nonetheless.

Nakazawa calls these chronic unpredictable toxic stress (CUTS) and describes some of the differences between men and women. She says, "Many women with a history of child-hood adversity develop a constellation of anxiety and depressive disorders, and autoimmune disease, and they do so in far great numbers than men."[6]

Further, the original ACE studies by Vincent Felitti, MD, and Robert Anda, MD, found that women are "50 percent more likely than men to have experienced five or more categories of Adverse Childhood Experiences." Felitti believes that "toxic childhood stress lies behind mainstream medicine's attitude that women are naturally prone to ill-defined health problems such as fibromyalgia, chronic fatigue syndrome, obesity, irritable bowel syndrome, and chronic pain."[7]

In my own research I've found a number of sex and gender differences. Males of all ages commit suicide at higher rates than females. I suspect this is related to the kinds of ACEs men experience and the lack of social supports that impacts so many men, particularly as we age.

Why Is This Important? The medical community has often overlooked the role of childhood trauma in explaining adult health problems. They prefer to give a host of medications that may address the symptoms, but they don't get at the actual cause of the problem. Psychiatrists and other mental health practitioners, who in the past looked in more depth at traumatic family history, now focus on giving drugs and ignoring the past. It may be quicker, but it guarantees that the root causes will never be treated, the patients will never fully recover, and they will have to return forever for treatment. That may not be the intent of individual practitioners, but it is the result of a system that ignores childhood abuse.

Step 6: Understand that childhood trauma undermines our adult relationships.

My wife, Carlin, and I have both had to deal with serious medical problems throughout our lives. She has suffered from chronic pain, migraines, and breast cancer. I have suffered from chronic anger, depression, and asthma. I've also had an adrenal tumor removed. We also have had numerous adverse childhood experiences. Both of us have been married twice before. Fortunately, we learned about the impact of childhood trauma and had done a good deal of therapeutic work before we got together.

Yet there was still a lot we didn't know and we fell into the trap that many couples deal with. For a lot of our marriage we were caught in a cycle of my anger leading to her withdrawal, which caused me to become angrier, which caused her to withdraw in order to protect herself. Like many couples who have numerous ACEs, these downward spirals were like rip tides that would grab us and pull us under when we least expected it.

Learning about the impact of our altered biology helped us be more tolerant of each other and more accepting of ourselves. It helped us to remain kind and generous, even when we were triggering each other's wounds.

Take a look again at ten ACEs and ten additional traumas and note the ones you checked. Ask yourself which ones may be having an impact on your relationship. For instance, it became clear to me that my father's absence and my mother's constant anxiety created reactions in me where I both craved Carlin's attention, but felt irritable and angry when she didn't respond in a way that I wanted.

For both of us, we were often on hyper-alert with each other. Any comment that seemed the least bit negative caused us to over-react, which would usually trigger an overreaction by the other. Even positive interactions might be viewed with suspicion. When I was feeling hurt or abandoned, I would interpret positive attempts at connection through a negative lens. As a result, neither of us would get the love we so desperately needed.

Step 7: Accept that trauma creates archetypal wounds and changes our self-perceptions.

The wounds we experience occur within the context of our family. Because we are children, dependent on our parents, we internalize the wounds. We can't blame our parents because to do so would endanger our very existence, so the wounds are taken into our bodies, minds, and spirits.

Neuropsychologist Mario Martinez, PhD, author of *The MindBody Code: How to Change the Beliefs That Limit Your Health, Longevity, and Success*, says there are three archetypal wounds that are experienced in cultures throughout the world:

- Abandonment.
- Shame.
- Betrayal.[8]

We internalize these wounds and they become part of the structure of our Mind/Body/Spirit. These experiences actually change the way our brains function and cause us to develop beliefs about ourselves that make us hunger for a relationship where we can heal, but also are triggered by stresses that arise in our relationships. Here are seven common self-limiting beliefs. Check off the ones you feel may be operating in your life today. You probably don't have these thoughts all the time, but they often play out in your subconscious, and act like a program running in the background, undermining your peace and well-being and coming out more strongly when you feel stressed.

1. I am not safe.
2. I am worthless.
3. I am powerless.
4. I am not loveable.
5. I cannot trust anyone.
6. I am bad.
7. I am alone.

I would often feel unsafe and untrusting. Carlin would often feel bad, that she couldn't ever do anything right. We both felt alone. We suffered mightily until we gradually began to heal our wounds. The good news is that we now know that these beliefs and the trauma that underlies them can be healed. Let me say it again; take a deep breath and let this sink in: These beliefs and the trauma that underlies them can be healed.

The fact that you are reading this book tells me that you are on a healing path. It takes courage and perseverance. It's never easy to heal these stubborn old wounds, but you will find that healing is a process. Sometimes progress will come with an instant change of perception, a change of heart. It's like a bright light shines through the darkness and you are illuminated. Healing can also come incrementally, little by little. Sometimes the progress is so slow you don't even know things are getting better. A friend or loved one may comment that you look happier, lighter—something has changed. However it comes, know that you are on the right path. I'll be with you all the way.

Step 8: Healing childhood trauma together is the greatest gift of love we can give and receive from each other.

In the introduction I suggested that the reason so many marriages fail is that we've been looking for love in all the wrong places using a faulty "love map." Because we don't understand that there are five stages to love, we think something's wrong when we hit stage 3 and must deal with confronting the childhood wounds that surface. We mistakenly believe the problem is with our partner or with ourselves.

We say we want "better communication, more love and understanding," but often we are looking for someone to blame for the pain we feel. We want to change them or change us. We become hooked on the negative image we see. During the falling-in-love and connecting phases we thought we were living with Prince Charming or "Princess Leah." In stage 3, we are suddenly confronted with the Wicked Witch. We are disoriented and confused.

Clients tell me:

- "I just want my husband back."
- "I love her, but I'm not *in love* with her anymore."
- "I don't feel seen, heard, loved, and respected."
- "I need to get away and sort things out. Something's missing here."

— "I don't know what's wrong, but I'm mad as hell
   most of the time."
— "Things are okay, but not great. I miss the passion,
   but maybe this is all there is."

But we're not really seeing our partner. We're looking at them through "trauma-colored glasses." Without realizing it, we're living in the past, re-experiencing childhood traumas. If we've been in a relationship before, we're also seeing the projection of the trauma we experienced in those relationships. It's as though our partner has become the abuser from our past. It's why so many men tell me, "I feel like she hates me. When I come into the room, I shrink under her hostile gaze." Women will say similar things: "He blames me for everything. I walk on eggshells when I'm around him. I can't do anything right."

Why Is This Important? Everything in life depends on context. If someone pulled your mouth open, stuck a needle in you, and caused you terrible pain, you might fight or flee. If the context is a dentist's office and you know the pain is temporary and the goal is to save your teeth, you accept the pain as part of the healing process. If we think the pain we are experiencing in our relationship means we're with the wrong person, we fight or flee. When we recognize that our partner is touching sensitive nerves so we can heal together, we accept the pain and appreciate that we're in stage 3 of marriage, not with the wrong partner.

Dr. Mario Martinez offers this insightful statement: "When we are wounded early by people we love, they teach us to entangle love with our wound."[9]

When I read these words, a lightbulb went off in my brain. Confusing life experiences fell into place. I thought, "That's why relationships seemed so crazy-making. One minute I would feel intense love and connection. The next minute I would want to kill the person I was with." I drove myself crazy trying to figure out which feeling was real. Is love real and the hate an illusion, or is the hate real and it's love that is the illusion? Should I stay and deepen the love, or should I get the hell out before one of us is killed?

There is a famous optical illusion I think of as "the beauty" or "the witch." Our brain can cause us to "flip" from one to the other. Traumatic wounds are always pulling us back to see the worst in our partner. Healing allows us to return to love. Once we understand that those who suffered from childhood trauma entangle love with our wound, we realize we're not crazy. We just need to heal the wounds and free the love.

Once we recognize that we're not seeing our loving partner—we're instead seeing the shadows of our past neglect, abuse, and abandonment—we can begin to heal them. What we need at this stage isn't a new partner. It isn't even marriage counseling to learn to communicate better. What we need is something quite different. We need to heal our traumatic wounds. We're really dealing with a kind of post-traumatic stress reaction, not a hopeless marriage.

The bad news is that the pain and confusion can totally disorient us. The good news is that we now have ways to heal these wounds so that we can get back on the track of real, lasting love. Here are some of the things I have found have worked for me and the men and women who have come to me for help over the years.

Understand that ACEs are real and allow ourselves to accept the truth of our wounds.

Just the act of reading this chapter, taking the ACE survey and looking at other childhood wounds are healing. Abuse, neglect, and abandonment grow stronger the more we deny them. Accepting our wounds can free our souls. "I always thought I had a happy childhood," a fifty-two-year-old man told me. "When I really accepted that I had been wounded I thought it would just pull me under and I'd be a puddle on the floor. Instead it has freed me and given me courage to heal more fully. For the first time I have hope that my relationship can be saved."

Get the pain out of your head and heart and down on paper.

Many people have told me that writing down memories of past trauma seems to help release the pain. "Just getting outside my body and writing it down on paper felt like a great relief," a forty-six-year-old woman told me. "It was as though the secrets that I had kept inside me in the dark were allowed to come out into the light. Ignoring the wounds only made me feel more like a victim. Acknowledging them has allowed me to take my power back."

Tell your partner, a close friend, or family member.

When we were kids we often didn't have anyone we could talk to. I remember having talks with my imaginary friends and sometimes with my dog. I longed to talk to another human being, but I felt there was no one I could talk to and as I child I didn't have the words to make sense of my fears, longings, and confusions. I've learned to open up to my wife and also to a number of my male friends. I was surprised that my experiences weren't unique. Others shared similar stories. Talking helps heal wounds.

Walk in nature.

Many people who have been wounded as children intuitively reach out for a connection in nature. I was a city kid, born in New York City, grew up in Los Angeles, and spent my adult life before moving to the country in the San Francisco Bay area. Since moving to the country, I've spend many healing hours in nature.

It may seem like a cliché, but I've become a tree hugger. There's something about the big trees here that heals the soul. Trees never seem to judge themselves or each other. They just stand tall and seem to exude a sense of peace and presence.

Find a good counselor.

In this book I'm sharing my heart and soul. I share what I would share with close friends and clients who come to me for help. But many people want and need to personal connection with a counselor who has gone through their own healing and can be a guide and mentor as you go through your own process. We all need different types of healing at different times of our lives. Follow your own intuition to connect with the right person at the right time for you.

In the next chapter we'll see that what we have assumed was incompatibility in our relationship, the feeling that we have grown apart, is really an invitation to go deeper. Rather than seeing these problems as indicators that something is wrong, we begin to see them as indicators that deep healing is in process.

Four

Incompatibility: Grounds for a Real Marriage, Not a Divorce

$\mathcal{I}$'ve counseled more than 25,000 couples over the last forty-plus years. Often both members of the couple are clearly unhappy, but usually one person makes a move that shakes things up. Sometimes it is an admission of an affair. Other times it is an angry outburst that is more extreme than usual. Sometimes one partner finds a text or e-mail that alerts them to the reality that their partner is involved with someone else. Other times it is a troubled statement of "I love you, but I'm not *in love* with you anymore. Something's gone out of our relationship, and I don't know if we can ever get it back."

Whatever the precipitating event, one or both partners come to the conclusion that "we're just not compatible anymore." The incompatibility may result in fighting or in boredom, but the conclusion is often "we're just too different to stay together." We live at a time where *togetherness* and *intimacy* are seen as core values. We often view *separation* and *distancing* as being dysfunctional in a healthy relationship.

Like the *disillusionment* we encounter in stage 3, *incompatibility* can be a good thing rather than grounds for divorce. "We've just grown apart," one man told me when he and his wife came for counseling. "We used to be close and in love, but now we just seem to have different needs and we are leading different lives." He saw this as proof that the marriage had lost the passion and power to remain intact. "I just think everyone would be better off if we admitted things were over between us. I'm sure I'll be a better father if there wasn't so much tension in the home." His wife disagreed: "I know we've grown apart, but I think we can get back to where we were. I want us to keep trying."

I've also seen these feelings expressed by the other sex. A woman came to see me to solicit my help in getting her husband to see why the marriage was over. "I've just lost all trust in him," she told me. "He tells me he'll do something, but he never follows through. If I can't trust him on the small stuff, how do I trust him to really be there when I need him? I've got my life to lead and he's pulling me down. I want out." When I interviewed her husband, he seemed completely beaten down. "I blame myself for a lot of our problems. I do have trouble keeping my word. I've become so focused on not doing anything wrong, I commit to things that I don't do. But I love my wife and I want to have the chance to make things better."

In working with both couples they were able to recognize that their incompatibility did not mean that things were hopeless or their marriage was over. I helped them understand the meaning of incompatibility in their marriage. Once they recognized that there was a chance they could be happy while remaining in the marriage, their perceptions began to shift and things began to improve.

I helped them see that incompatibility was actually a good thing. They could take a step back and re-evaluate their lives and where they wanted to go. When they weren't so focused on getting closer and regaining intimacy, they could breathe more easily. They could re-frame their relationship challenges:

Old Frame: We've grown apart. We're really different people. We just don't have that much in common. Whenever I try to get close to you, you just pull away. When you want to be close to me, it's the last thing I want. We're incompatible. Let's just admit it, go our separate ways, and get on with our lives.

New Frame: We're at a time in our lives when we are recognizing new aspects of ourselves. The old-me fit well with the old-you. But I'm a different person now. I'm growing and changing, and I don't want to be tied to old ways of being or even to an old relationship. We're incompatible. Let's just admit it and allow ourselves to grow into the person we are at this stage of our lives. Maybe we'll even find we want to scrap our old marriage and create a new one that fits better for us.

Step 1: Understand that incompatibility is not grounds for divorce, but the beginning of real, lasting love.

When I tell this to clients they are confused and disoriented. They come in believing that all the fighting or silent distancing is an indicator that the couple is incompatible and should separate. I tell them the opposite. Their incompatibility is really a good thing. It is telling them they are ready to let go of the illusions that their hopes and dreams of happiness have been solved when they met that special someone and fell in love. It also alerts them that things are changing and they need a new perspective on love and marriage.

Once they understand, a change occurs. They feel less frightened. Usually one member of the partnership understands these issues before the other. It's not unusual for either the man or the woman to feel doubtful. One man told me, "I'm not convinced by what you're saying. Things feel awful and I don't think things can really change. Our personalities are just different. I may still decide to leave and I don't want my wife to get her hopes up that

I'm going to stay." His wife wished he were more positive, but she was willing to keep the faith and move ahead.

Why Is This Important? Most of us have grown up with the romantic notion that a good marriage is close and loving. But in an enlightened marriage we can appreciate and accept that a good marriage can include closeness as well as distance, compatibility and incompatibility. Love and intimacy can occur as we move toward each other. They can also occur as we move away. It's good to feel the things we have in common with our partner, but it's also good to feel the freedom of our unique, separate selves.

Step 2: Realize that the pain of incompatibility triggers dark nights of the soul.

When Carlin and I reached stage 3, I can remember many nights lying awake, feeling miserable and confused. I felt lost and abandoned, and I wondered how things had gone so wrong. We just couldn't seem to get on the same page on anything. I hurt her and she hurt me. I questioned the marriage. I questioned my life.

Over the many months and years we struggled, we both were drawn down into what was clearly a spiritual crisis. The phrase "dark night of the soul" comes from the Spanish mystic and poet John of the Cross (1541–1597). John was a member of the Christian religious order of Carmelites and, along with St. Teresa of Avila, tried to reform the order. He was imprisoned and from his search for meaning came poems of deep beauty and wisdom and his concept of healing and re-awakening through emotional trials.

Stages 1 and 2 of marriage are mostly sweetness and light. But later things become darker and more intense. For long periods of time we ignore the changes. We are busy with work, busy with family. We hope that things will fall into place and we can return to the time of our lives when we were passionate with each other and love flowed easily.

If we stay on a superficial level we can think we just need a superficial change. We try and enliven our sex lives or take a vacation. But the "dark night" pulls us down. We are unprepared and don't understand what is going on. It's easy to think the problem is with our spouse. One man went on and on about the problems with his wife. **After listening to him it became clear that the problem wasn't with his wife. It was with his life.** If we don't run away, we realize the dark night of the soul is our chance to put our trust in the "power of two," to stay with our partner and go deeper.

Why Is This Important? When we run up against our incompatibilities, we are getting closer to our true selves. Master-mythologist and writer Joseph Campbell explored these issues in the posthumously published *Pathways to Bliss: Mythology and Personal Transformation.* Campbell captures the process that so many encounter, but fail to fully understand. He says:

> Two people meet and fall in love. Then they marry, and the real Sam or Suzy begins to show through the fantasy, and, boy, is it a shock. They get a divorce and wait for another receptive person, pitch the woo again, and, uh-oh, another shock. And so on and so forth.
>
> Now the one undeniable fact: this disillusion is inevitable. You had an ideal. You married that ideal, then along comes a fact that does not correspond to that ideal. You suddenly notice things that do not quite fit with your projection. So what are you going to do when that happens?
>
> There's only one attitude that will solve the situation: compassion. This poor, poor fact that I married does not correspond to my ideal; it's only a human being. Well, I'm a human being, too. So I'll meet a human being for a change; I'll live with it and be nice to it, showing compassion for the fallibilities that I myself have certainly brought

to life as a human being." It takes courage to let go of our illusions and learn to love a real, live, human being with flaws as beautiful and maddening as our own.[1]

Now we recognize that marriage is not about "living happily ever after." It is a serious spiritual journey, a hero's journey, and is triggered by a "dark night of the soul." Not everyone is ready for the journey, but when it calls to us, we need to step up and take the plunge.

Step 3: Accept that 90 percent of our conflicts come from our past, not our present.

Most of us believe that whatever problems we had in the past have little to do with our present relationship. Childhood losses may have been painful, but now that we're adults we believe we have outgrown them. We also believe that wounds and disappointments from previous relationships need not be addressed because we're with a new partner. We are sure we left the problems behind us when we ended the earlier relationship and are now with the "right" partner. But as we begin to feel unhappy once again, we question whether we are really with the right person.

As we feel our pain and unhappiness increasing, we blame our partner. Whether voiced out loud or merely thought to ourselves, we are full of a litany of "if onlys."

- If only you'd listen to me.
- If only you turned me on like you used to do.
- If only you'd talk to me about what you're *really* feeling.
- If only you'd get help for your depression.

The list goes on and on, and we become unhappier and unhappier.

But the truth is most of our unhappiness is not about our partner. In fact, 90 percent of our conflicts come from the past. According to marriage and family experts Harville Hendrix and his wife, Helen LaKelly Hunt, "Since partnership is designed to resurface feelings from childhood, it means that most of the upset that gets triggered in us during our relationship is from our past."

Even when we recognize that our present unhappiness might be tied to a previous relationship, the ultimate root of the problem actually goes back to childhood. "About 90 percent of the frustrations your partner has with you are really about *their* issues from childhood," say Hendrix and Hunt. "That means only 10 percent or so is about each of you right now."

Why Is This Important? The root feelings of incompatibility *are not* the result of problems with our partner or with ourselves. This can give real hope to those who are in pain. Instead of blaming our partner or wishing they were different, we can focus on the issues from our past that are triggering problems in the present. In this way we can solve problems once and for all. We can avoid going through a painful divorce, only to find ourselves in the same situation with another partner.

Step 4: Recognize the connection between chronic problems with our spouse and past wounds from our parents.

When one or both members of the couple conclude that "we're just not compatible," it usually follows years of chronic unhappiness. There are usually themes or behaviors that demonstrate that "we're really too different to remain together." Here are some of the common themes I hear from my clients. Which ones resonate with you?

— I want more sex, but my spouse just isn't that interested anymore.

— I want to go out and have fun, but my spouse just
  wants to stay at home at watch TV.
— I want more time for *us*, but my spouse is so
  wrapped up in work I feel I'm just not that important.
— Now that the children are mostly grown we just
  don't have that much in common.
— The fire has gone out of the relationship. What's left
  is cold and lifeless. I want my life back.

These issues often are reflected in beliefs we have about ourselves, including the following:

— I am not loveable.
— I am worthless.
— I am powerless.
— I am not safe.
— I cannot trust anyone.
— I am bad.
— I am alone.

Recall from Chapter 3 that these are the beliefs that arise from
the wounds we experienced as children. Think back about the
frustrations you had with your parents or other caregivers from
your childhood and see how many relate to frustrations you've
been having with your spouse. You may wish to write these down.

It was a revelation for me when I did this exercise and saw
that one of my main complaints about Carlin was that she would
withdraw from me when I needed her love and support. I would
get angry. She would insist that the reason she withdrew was
that I would get angry and push her away. I would insist that I
only got angry when I felt hurt that she was distancing herself
from me.

I immediately recognized my parents' dynamic. My mother
was frightened of my father's anger and she'd withdraw. He felt
emotionally abandoned and would become increasingly irritated

and angry. Once I began looking I found that nearly all our conflicts and incompatibilities had roots in childhood.

Why Is This Important? Many of the issues that recur in our present marriage and cause us to despair at having a good relationship are actually tied to the past. Once we recognize the real source of our conflicts, a lot of our problems now make sense. Instead of endless loops of misunderstandings that never seem to resolve, we now can see that by healing our old wounds we can heal our marriage and that by healing our marriage we are able to heal our childhood wounds once and for all.

Step 5: Accept that under stress one of you closes like a clam while the other screeches like an angry seagull.

There seem to be two major energies in life. Anthropologist Angeles Arrien called them the "Dynamic" and the "Magnetic."[2] The dynamic has an outward thrust. The magnetic has an equally powerful energy pulling inwards. When we're under stress we each have a characteristic way of dealing with it. I call it the "Clam" and the "Seagull."

When Carlin is stressed she tends to withdraw. She closes down like a clam. She doesn't want to talk. Her energy goes inwards. When I'm stressed I want to talk about it. I fly off the handle and become frenzied. For many years we each thought our response was *logical* and *right* and our partner's response was *illogical* and *wrong*. We were also blind to the impact that our response had on our partner.

I would be upset, scared, or hurt, and I would want to talk about it. If Carlin didn't listen closely and compassionately I would get upset and angry. I felt she didn't care about me, that she wasn't interested in hearing me or supporting me. It took me a long time to realize that she felt overwhelmed by my *seagull energy*. She felt pecked at and attacked. She would go into her shell and shut down. Her withdrawal frightened me, and I'd try harder and harder to get through to her. I'd fly back and forth trying to get her to come out of her shell and listen to me.

These endless interactions left us both exhausted. We each felt uncared for and worn down. If we hadn't recognized that we each had a different reaction to stress, we would have concluded that we were with the wrong partner. Once we did recognize it, we could better accept our partner's style and help ease their pain rather than adding to it. Do you recognize yourself and your partner here? Of course there are times that clams can act like seagulls and vice versa, but usually there is a preference for one over the other.

Just knowing and accepting these differences can help. But we can also go further and understand and support the other's needs:

Clams seek safety when stressed and turn inward. They want to be free from the demands of painful interactions. They need to think and sort out what's going on, lick their wounds, and find nourishment though self-reflection.

Seagulls thrive on contact. They want to talk things out, be touched and held. They are often terrified of being alone and can scream loudly when they feel they are not getting the attention they need.

Once we understand our characteristic reactions, we can be more supportive of our partner. We can also learn from our partner. Finding true health and balance in life means becoming more like our partner. I learned the value of taking time to myself and the ability to self-nurture. Carlin has learned to reach out for care and nurture and she can give it more easily. She has learned to talk more about her needs, and reach out when she was stressed and I've learned to talk less and listen more.

Why Is This Important? The Dynamic/Magnetic (Seagull/Clam) difference is one of our core incompatibilities. It's also one of the main reasons we are together. Both types need to learn from the other. Like many incompatibilities, these can be a source of growth and strength. For instance, to help a clam come out of their shell, we can give them time and space, and trust that if left alone they will peek their head out soon. Seagulls need contact. Asking a stressed seagull, "How can I help? Is there something I can do?" immediately quiets them and they feel cared for. We can each learn to grow in our partnership through our incompatibilities.

Step 6: Know that one person must make a commitment on behalf of the couple.

Rarely do both members of a couple arrive together at the realization that they want to recommit to improving their relationship. Usually one person gets there first. Because we're conditioned to believe that "it takes two people to make a relationship work," the person who is most aware of the need may be discouraged about committing to the relationship if their partner doesn't seem interested in making a similar commitment.

One of my most popular articles is titled "5 Secrets for Saving Your Midlife Marriage, Even if Only One of You Is Trying to Keep it Alive." In it I say, "After working with men and women for more than 40 years, I've found that it only takes one person who is committed to the relationship to turn things around."[3]

When someone comes to see me who is concerned about their relationship going under, but truly wants to keep it alive, I ask them to make a time commitment to make things better. At first they may feel reluctant. "How can I make things better if my spouse refuses to get help?"

I remind them that we are all connected and couples are deeply connected. Think of yourself as being attached to your partner by a rope connecting your centers. If you move one way, your partner will feel the pull. Likewise, if you make a commitment to the relationship and begin to change your own responses, you will find that your partner will feel it and the downward spiral of your dysfunctional relationship will turn around. You may see the effect immediately, or it may take time for your partner to respond positively to your pull. Often wounds are so deep that even when things change for the better we are reluctant to trust them. Don't give up. Hang in there. Your changes can, and will, impact your partner for the better.

My guess is that if you are reading this book you have a strong desire to do everything you can to understand what is going on in your relationship and do everything you can to help it grow stronger. I'd ask you to make an effort to get your relationship back on a positive track. There's much you can do. Think beyond yourself and even your partner. Think of the relationship itself. Most people don't want to give up on their relationship even when things are difficult. On the other hand, most people aren't willing to live "until death do us part" in a relationship that is destructive.

If you were coming to me as a client I would tell you that it takes some time to begin to turn things around. A relationship, in this respect, is like a big ocean liner. It takes some time to change course. So I'll ask you to make a commitment to give 100 percent of your efforts to improving the relationship, no matter how committed or not committed your partner is. I'll also ask you to attach a time stamp.

One client said, "I'm 100 percent committed to making things better, and I'm willing to give it a year to do everything I can to improve things for the better." Another told me, "I'm 80 percent committed, but I've been going through so much pain and betrayal I'm not sure how long I can keep trying." With some additional discussion and guidance, I got this commitment: "I know I can commit to staying with the relationship at least until the end of the month."

Whatever time you feel you can commit to is fine for this step. Whether it's long term or short term doesn't matter. You can always extend the period, because I check in with people at the end of this period.

Write down your time commitment. This has two purposes: It lets you know that you have some time to learn new skills and to put into practice what you are learning from the book. It also lets you know that the commitment isn't forever. I guarantee that you will begin to see improvements if you continue following these steps.

Why Is This Important? Many people who come to me are discouraged because their partner has told them directly or indirectly that he or she feels the relationship has no future. "I want the relationship with all my heart," one woman told me, "but he refuses to get help. I guess I'll just have to accept his decision and move on." A man told me, "My wife says it's the last straw. She's unhappy with our life together and wants to move on. I guess there's nothing I can do."

No, I tell them. It's never over until both of you have decided it's over. As long as one person is still in the game, there is hope. I've seen literally hundreds of relationships turn around because one person remained committed, got help, and made things better for both partners.

Step 7: Come to peace with the reality that all relationships end. The question is when and how.

All relationships end. Some end in divorce. Others end in the death of a spouse. Some end when the couple gives up hope of love and simply remains together as housemates. Others end with a death and rebirth of the relationship with the same person.

No one says, "I'm madly in love, intensely bonded with my partner, and joyfully alive. I think I'll get a divorce." If not through actual death of a spouse, most relationships end during this time of incompatibility. As I've said, not only do I think this is not a good reason to end the relationship, but I believe it is the best reason to move ahead and go deeper.

The satisfaction of stage 4 lies ahead with all its mystery and meaning. But not everyone wants to engage in this journey. Truly some people should get out of the relationship. There are times when the abuse and neglect from childhood results in abuse and neglect in this relationship. There's a lot one person can do, but sometimes the spouse is so locked in their anger and pain and so unwilling to get help, the only option is to leave. But I believe that with guidance and support most marriages can be healed.

According to Thomas Merton, one of the most profound spiritual writers of our time, "The beginning of love is the will to let those we love be perfectly themselves, the resolution not to twist them to fit our own image. If in loving them we do not love what they are, but only their potential likeness to ourselves, then we do not love them: we only love the reflection of ourselves we find in them."[4] Too many of us seek a superficial happiness and run when we are asked to go deeper. My message to most is this:

Don't give up. Don't leave too soon. The best is yet to come.

Why Is This Important? I tell my clients that whether they stay together or leave the marriage, the old relationship is over. In the past we suffered, hurt ourselves, and hurt each other. We didn't know what was causing the pain so we blamed ourselves or our partner. We wanted to get the pain to stop and we thought the only way we could do that was to get out of the relationship or deaden the pain by closing down all our feelings. Now we know there is a different path and we can commit to creating a new relationship.

Step 8: Understand that the journey to real, lasting love is not for everyone.

Although we all have the capacity to engage all five stages of love, the complete journey is not for everyone. It requires a certain level of maturity that can only occur, I believe, to people who are over forty. But age is not the only factor. Life experience counts as well. Some forty-year-olds are ready to do the healing work necessary for love to deepen and grow. Others may not be ready until they are in their fifties, sixties, or seventies.

Further, some people are more open than others to addressing the wounds from childhood. For some the pain is so great they just can't bring themselves to deal with it. We recognize this process with alcoholics and addicts who are beginning work to recover. For some they go back to their drinking or drugging because they just aren't yet ready to deal with the pain. I don't see that as a failure. Everyone must find their own time to address these problems.

One person's readiness and commitment to the relationship can give the other person the support they need to make their own commitment. That's why I encourage people who stick with it, even if their partner doesn't yet seem ready. But I also encourage the person to have their own time commitment. I've had some clients who were willing to work for years, even if their partner wasn't ready. Others would do it only for months before they decided they needed to move on.

Why Is This Important? I tell people not to leave too soon. But I also tell them that despite their best intentions and desires, sometimes their partner isn't ready to do the work of healing within a time frame that they can live with. I've seen some couples who are able to work together and get their relationship back on track, even when only one of them was committed from the beginning. I've seen couples who split up, went their separate ways, did their individual healing work, and remarried years later. I've also seen couples who went their separate ways, did their healing, and found the love of their lives the second or third time around. The best we can hope for is to have compassion for ourselves and our partner as we go through this miraculous and sometimes-confusing journey we call life.

In the next chapter you'll learn more about men and women and the wonderful dance that makes sex and love so interesting and engaging.

Five

Why Sex Matters: Men and Women Coming Together

There was a time in the 1950s when it seemed clear what it meant to be a man and what it meant to be a woman. Men went away to work and women stayed home to take care of the children. Men spent their free time in the garage fixing cars and repairing things around the house. Women cooked our meals in the kitchen and spent time socializing with other women and fixing our scraped knees and bruised feelings. On TV we learned about men, women, and families from *Father Knows Best*, and *Leave it to Beaver* introduced us to June and Ward, the perfect couple with perfect kids Wally and the cute and clever Beaver Cleaver. Life was simple. Life was good.

Of course real life wasn't like that. I was an only child, and my father had a nervous breakdown when I was five. He and my mother got divorced and she had to leave the home to work every day. I learned to take care of myself, but I hungered for the *real* family I thought everyone else had. Though I didn't have the real-life family role models of the traditional father and mother, I learned the qualities I "knew" were the ones that "real men" and "real women" should aspire toward. There was a *man's world* and there was a *woman's world* and they were not only separate, but opposite.

For instance, growing up I learned that *men must be* and *women must not be*:

— The primary breadwinner.
— Physically strong.
— Good with tools.
— Logical.
— Hairy.
— Aggressive.
— Muscular.
— Tough.
— Hard.
— Decisive.

The reverse was also true. I learned that *women must be* and *men must not be*:

— Home with the kids.
— Weak.
— Emotional.
— Smooth.
— Passive.
— Curvy.
— Tender.
— Soft.
— Yielding.

Why Is This Important? This is important for a couple of reasons. First, many of us still carry these stereotypes in our subconscious. Even though we may tell ourselves that men don't always have to be the breadwinner or that women aren't always emotional, our subconscious may still believe it and limit how we see ourselves or our partner. Second, some of these differences, which we assume are just superficial, may actually tap into deeper roots of sex differences that are part of our gender identity.

In reaction to these stereotypes that didn't fit our actual experience, we went in the opposite direction. We decided that dividing the world into simple categories of "male" and "female" didn't work well. Women refused to limit their identity to stay-at-home moms, and men broke under the pressures to always be strong and hard at the expense of being gentle and emotional. Both men and women had to, and wanted to, work outside the home; and both men and women wanted a more engaged relationship with their children. Further, recognizing and accepting lesbian, gay, bisexual, and transgender (LGBT) individuals further expanded our ideas of what it meant to be male and female.

The view of sex and gender roles began to expand greatly. Many believed that the differences between males and females was superficial, simply based on how we were raised and the social stereotypes that we were taught. We thought it was much better to raise our children as "people." When I had kids I wanted my little girl to play with trucks as well as dolls and for my son to learn to express his tender feelings, not just his anger. This was a good thing and has allowed everyone to express who they truly are. But like all reactions, we often go too far.

We are now learning that there are real differences in males and females and that we're entering a new era where we can learn to respect our differences as well as our similarities. In order to be whom we are and to have relationships that are able to generate real, lasting love, we need to learn about the new field of Gender-Specific Medicine.

After recognizing the ways in which heart-attack symptoms and risk differed between men and women, Marianne J. Legato, MD, FACP, founded the Foundation for Gender-Specific Medicine in 2006. According to Dr. Legato, "Until now, we've acted as though men and women were essentially identical except for the differences in their reproductive function. In fact, information we've been gathering over the past ten years tells us that this is anything but true, and that everywhere we look, the two sexes are startingly and unexpectedly different not only in their normal function but in the ways they experience illness."[1] Dr. Legato's discoveries and those of her colleagues have led to a personalization of medicine that assists healthcare practitioners worldwide in understanding the difference in normal function of men and women and in their sex-specific experiences of the same diseases.

Step 1: Understand the essence of male and female.

As we all know, life begins with an egg and a sperm. This may be the ultimate power of two. There are important, little-appreciated realities about this simple act of creation that will help us better understand ourselves and our partners.

Biologists have a very simple and useful definition of what is male and what is female, whether we are fish, ferns, or human beings. An individual can either make many small gametes (sex cells) or fewer but larger gametes. The individuals that produce smaller gametes are called *males* and the ones that produce larger gametes are called *females*.

About 400 eggs are ovulated in a woman's lifetime. A healthy male produces 500 million sperm per day. A single human female egg, for instance, is so large it could house 250,000 sperm.

Why Is This Important? The fact that the egg is larger and scarcer means that sperm will have to compete to gain access to the valuable eggs. Because women are the ones who carry the developing fetus in their womb, they commit much more than do men to the evolutionary success of the species. A male can deposit a bit of sperm and move on. Like the egg they carry, women choose which man she will marry. As a result, males will compete with other males for access to the most valuable females. According to evolutionary psychology theory, this difference results in men and women pursuing different "reproductive strategies." As we'll see, our differing genetics, our brain function, our hormones, and even our communication all work together to guide men and women to different, yet complementary ways of relating.

Step 2: Realize that every cell in our body is sex specific.

According to David C. Page, MD, professor of biology at the Massachusetts Institute of Technology (MIT), there are 10 trillion cells in the human body and every one of them is sex specific. Here's why: The egg can only carry an X chromosome, but some sperm carry the Y and some carry the X.[2] We all start out as a single cell, and each cell has twenty-three sets of chromosomes. We get one of each pair from our mother in the egg, and one of each pair from our father in the sperm. The first twenty-two pairs are labeled longest to shortest. The last pair are called the sex chromosomes, labeled X or Y. If we are female, every cell in our body carries an XX pair of chromosomes. If we are male, every cell in our body carries an XY pair of chromosomes (except for those who have a genetic anomaly).

Why Is This Important? Recent scientific findings are demonstrating that these cellular differences can make a big difference in everything, from how our brains work to who we choose as a mate, from which hormones predominate in our lives to how we talk and listen to each other. "So all your cells know, on a molecular level, whether they are XX or XY," says Dr. Page. "It is true that a great deal of the research going on today which seeks to understand the causes and treatments for disease is failing to account for this most fundamental difference between men and women. The study of disease is flawed."[3]

Step 3: Recognize that sex differences matter more than we once believed.

We once thought that the differences just had to do with our sexual organs. Some doctors described it as "bikini medicine." But new research is showing that differences are much more important than we once believed.

Here's one real-life example of how these sex differences can impact our lives.

Larry Cahill, a neuroscientist at the University of California, Irvine, admits that like many fellow scientists, he used to think men and women were fundamentally the same outside the obvious areas of reproduction and sex hormones. But he and many others have changed their minds. On a special report on CBS's *60 Minutes,* he reported that Ambien, the well-known sleep medication, which was approved in 1992, is a case in point. We now know that women metabolize Ambien differently, reaching maximum blood levels 45 percent higher than those of men.

"That is a textbook example of what is wrong," said Cahill. "How did it happen that for 20 some years, women, millions of them, were essentially overdosing on Ambien?" This may be true for many other drugs. And the reverse may also be true. While women are getting too much of a medication, men may not be getting enough.[4] Cahill thinks science needs to rethink the importance of sex differences and study them from the earliest stages of animal research, including reviewing existing drugs. Knowing there are many differences and still operating on the assumption the sexes are the same must change, he says. "So the assumption we're making, that sex really doesn't matter, is not a valid assumption," he says. "It may not matter. It may matter hugely . . . the way we're doing business has to change."[5]

Step 4: Accept that males and females are more different than we once thought.

Dr. Legato launched the Foundation for Gender-Specific Medicine to gather and conduct research on ways to improve our health by understanding sex differences in men and women. She concludes, "Men and women think differently, approach problems differently, emphasize the importance of things differently, and experience the world around us through entirely different filters."[6] This research has implications not only for our physical, mental, and spiritual health, but on the essence of our sex and love lives. For instance, Dr. Page has found that men and women are much more different genetically than we had ever recognized. It has been said that our genomes are 99.9 percent identical from one person to the next. "It turns out that this assertion is correct," says Dr. Page, "as long as the two individuals being compared are both men. It's also correct if the two individuals being compared are both women. However, if you compare the genome of a man with the genome of a woman, you'll find that they are only 98.5% identical."

"In other words," says Dr. Page, "the genetic difference between a man and a woman are 15 times greater than the genetic difference between two men or between two women."[7] [Note: This is a 0.1 percent difference between two men or two women and a 1.5 percent difference between a man and a woman; if that doesn't seem like a lot, remember the human genome is only 1.5-percent different from the chimpanzee genome.]

Why Is This Important? It puts to rest the idea that we can ignore sex differences. If we want to learn to love ourselves and our partner, we need to accept that we are different and learn to appreciate and work with the differences, not try to artificially create a gender-neutral way of being in the world. When *different* meant "less than" or "worse than" we could understand why some would want to insist that we are all the same. But now we must recognize that we are different and our differences can be the source of passion and joy.

Step 5: Appreciate that male and female brains are different.

Like every other part of us, the male and female brains are significantly different.

Louann Brizendine, MD, is a professor of clinical psychiatry at the University of California, San Francisco and codirector of the UCSF Program in Sexual Medicine. She was previously on the faculty at the Harvard Medical School and is a graduate of the Yale University School of Medicine. She's written two engaging books, appropriately titled *The Female Brain* and *The Male Brain*. Here are some differences she found that can help us better understand why men and women are the way they are:

- In the brain centers for language and hearing, women have 11 percent more neurons than men.
- The principal hub of both emotion and memory formation—the hippocampus—is also larger in the female brain, as is the brain circuitry for language and observing emotions in others.
- Men, by contrast, have two and a half times the brain space devoted to sexual drive as well as larger brain centers for action and aggression.
- Sexual thoughts float through a man's brain every fifty-two seconds on average, and through a woman's only once a day. Perhaps three to four times on her hottest days.

Dr. Marianne J. Legato describes many of these, and other differences, in her well-titled book, *Why Men Never Remember and*

Women Never Forget.[8] "There's some evidence (as the very title of this book suggests)," says Dr. Legato, "that women have better memories than men do for the spoken word." Women also have higher levels of estrogen than do men and this is also a key difference between the sexes. "Estrogen is also an element in a key finding," says Legato, "that women remember stressful events better than men do."

Why Is This Important? It's often difficult to see the world through the eyes of another. It can be even more difficult when we are looking out of the world from a brain that may be very different. Knowing about these differences can help us to withhold judgment of ourselves and our partner. I often get frustrated when Carlin seems to throw a wet blanket on my new ideas because she worries about everything that could go wrong. It helps to remind myself that she more readily remembers stressful events from the past and hence worries more than I do about potential failures.

Step 6: Recognize that the hormonal balance is different in men and women.

Understanding the difference in the male and female brains are related to differences in our hormones. "Hormones," says Dr. Brizendine, "can determine what the brain is interested in doing. They help guide nurturing, social, sexual, and aggressive behaviors."[9] I always thought of "hormones" as something that affected women, but had little to do with men. One of the first jokes I heard as a kid when I was nine or ten years old: "Do you know how to make a hormone?" I wasn't sure what a hormone was and I had no idea how to make one. I was totally confused by the punch line. "Don't pay her!" My older buddy laughed uproariously and I laughed along.

When I entered puberty I felt even more confused with the changes going on in my body and knew they had something to do with hormones. Most of us have heard more jokes about hormones than facts.

My colleague, Theresa L. Crenshaw, MD, was one of the world's leading experts on sexuality and the ways hormones influence our love lives. She cowrote a textbook *Sexual Pharmacology*, and a popular book based on her research, *The Alchemy of Love and Lust: Discovering Our Sex Hormones and How They Determine Who We Love, When We Love, and How Often We Love.* In the introduction she clearly states a concern I share with her: **"It's appalling, but a seemingly trivial lack of information about hormones can destroy a marriage."**

She says if we are to have a healthy sex and love life, we have to be aware of the players in our internal hormonal symphony, or as she calls them, **The Love Brigade.** "When you fall in love or lust it is not merely an emotional event," she says. "Your various hormones get in bed with you too." Next time you are with your lover, be aware of your bed partners. Here some of the most important members of the brigade.[10]

Oxytocin

Oxytocin has been called the "cuddle hormone" or the "love hormone," but it is much more than that. It can intensify memories of poor bonding, like those we might have of an absent father or an angry mother. Whether it makes us feel cuddly or suspicious toward our partner depends on our previous experiences.

The social nature of oxytocin operates differently in men and women. In men it improves the ability to identify competitive relationships and enables them to punish those who violate the rules of society. In studies, those who cheat are punished more often by males. In females, oxytocin facilitates the ability to identify kinship. Oxytocin enables women to be more under-standing and to smooth over social conflicts.

Oxytocin promotes empathy. According to researcher Paul J. Zak, PhD, author of *The Moral Molecule: The Source of Love and Prosperity,* "When oxytocin goes up, he or she responds more generously and caringly, even with complete strangers."[11]

Vasopressin

Vasopressin has been called the monogamy molecule. Prairie voles, like humans, form strong pair-bonds. But when given a drug that blocks the effect of vasopressin, the bond with their partner deteriorates and they become more promiscuous.

Serotonin

Many of us know about serotonin from ads for antidepressants. Keeping our serotonin up can reduce feelings of sadness and keep us from obsessing. Lower serotonin levels are associated with the preoccupation we have with our partner when we're newly in love. In fact, serotonin levels of new lovers were found to be similar to the low serotonin levels of obsessive-compulsive disorder patients. A downside of taking antidepressants may be loss of that wonderful, but crazy, obsessing we do when we fall in love.

Dopamine

Dopamine is the neurotransmitter that stimulates the reward center in the brain and is associated with pursuit of pleasure. It is the driving force in all addictions, whether to drugs, sex, or romance. It has a similar effect in the brain as cocaine. Not only does it focus our desire for our partner, but it gives us the energy to pursue them.

Estrogen

Estrogen is important for sexual desire. We often think of estrogen as the female hormone, but it is present in males and females. In fact, older men often have more estrogen than older women and it accounts for men's softening, gentling, and greater emotional sensitivity as we age. I say that men get more "esty" as we age, but balancing estrogen with testosterone is important throughout life.

Testosterone

We think of testosterone as the male sex hormone that makes men horny and makes them aggressively pursue sex. But testosterone is also important for women's sex and love life. Loss of libido in women often is caused by lowering testosterone levels. Estrogen levels drop more than testosterone levels as women age and helps account for women's greater assertiveness as they get older. I say women become more "testy" as they age.

These hormones evolved in men and women to help us survive and thrive during our long history as hunter–gatherers. Although both males and females make all these hormones, they are made in different amounts and have different effects.

On average, in adult males, levels of testosterone are about seven to eight times higher than in adult females. This helps account for males' continual interest in sex, sexual variety, and aggression.

Testosterone blocks the binding of oxytocin to its receptor sites. So men, with their higher testosterone levels, are less prone to be empathic than females.

Why Is This Important? Understanding the power of hormones and how they influence our lives can help us feel better about ourselves and our partner. It makes it easier for us to get beyond questions of "who is right and who is wrong." We stop thinking of men as having "testosterone poisoning" or "oxytocin as the love hormone." When we recognize the evolutionary value of the different ways men and women survive and thrive it allows us to appreciate ourselves as males and females. It also alerts us to deal with the changes that occur as we age and hormone balance shifts.

Step 7: Honor the fact that there are exceptions to every rule, including what is male and what is female.

I'm sure as I've described the differences between men and women, some of you have thought, "Right on, that's exactly how me and my spouse are." Others, I'm sure, have thought, "Wait a minute, that's doesn't seem right to me." When we talk about male/female differences there are always exceptions to the rule. To fully appreciate ourselves and our partner we need to explore both the rule and the exception

Here's a little thought experiment that I've found helpful. Imagine that you have $1,000 and you're going to play a game. With each round you place a bet of $100. At the end of the game, we double whatever money you've won. You want to come out of the game with the most money. Here we go: Behind the curtain is either a man or a woman, selected at random from a group of 100 women and 100 men. All I can tell you is that the person is more than 6 feet tall. You will bet $100 on whether the person is a man or a woman. If you are right you win $100. If you are wrong you lose $100. Most people would bet that the person behind the curtain is a man, and you'd likely win some money. Most people more than 6 feet tall are men, though there are, of course, some women more than 6 feet tall.

If we repeated the experiment and told you the person behind the curtain was less than 5 feet 5 inches tall. You'd probably bet that you'd see a woman coming out. But you might lose your bet when I came out from behind the curtain and stretched to my full height of 5 feet 4 inches tall. On the scale of height, I don't fit the rule.

Let's stick with me for a little longer to illustrate another place where there are exceptions to the rule. Simon Baron-Cohen, PhD, is one of the world's leading experts on sex differences between men and women. In his book *The Essential Difference: The Truth About the Male & Female Brain*, he wastes no time addressing these differences. In the first paragraph of the book he says, "The subject of essential sex differences in the mind is clearly very delicate. I could tiptoe around it, but my guess is that you would like the theory of the book stated plainly.[12] Here it is:

"The female brain is predominantly hard-wired for empathy. The male brain is predominantly hard-wired for understanding and building systems."

Baron-Cohen goes on to describe the differences, and at the end of the book he includes a Systemizing Quotient (SQ) scale to determine the degree an individual has a male-dominant brain and an Empathy Quotient Scale (EQ) to determine the degree an individual has a female-dominant brain. He notes that both men and women empathize and systematize, but usually women predominate in the former and males in the latter.

When I filled out the questionnaire and got my score, I was not surprised when I scored very high on the Empathy scale. It fits well with my chosen profession as a therapist. Nor was I surprised when I scored low on the Systematizing Scale. I'm terrible at fixing things, I have no interest in "manly tools," and I'd much prefer my wife drive than me. (She also knows much more about fixing cars than I do.)

I was surprised, however, that I scored higher on the Empathy Scale than most women and I scored lower on the Systematizing Scale, not only than most men, but actually lower than most women. Even though I consider myself an "All-American Man," my brain functions in many ways more like a woman's. And at systematizing, I don't even measure up to most women.

Why Is This Important? The purpose of this chapter and really the purpose of the whole book is to help us get more in touch with who we really are. Sometimes who we really are will fit the predominate experience of most people of our sex, sometimes it will be the opposite, and most often it will fall somewhere in between. Further, these differences will likely change over time. As we age, we may shift and become more yin or more yang. I like using these ancient Chinese symbols because they recognize that we all have a mixture of "masculine" and "feminine" traits, and our goal, ultimately, is to accept ourselves and each other for who we are and learn to love more deeply.

Six

Male and Female Communication With and Without Words: Bridging the Great Divide

I had an "aha" experience when I recognized that I talk very differently when I interact with my wife than when I'm talking to close male friends. When Carlin and I talk there's a certain tension. Although we've learned to communicate better and better through the years, I feel like our interaction is more like speaking a second language, rather than what is natural to me. I sense the same is true for her as well.

When I overhear her talking with female friends on the phone, they seem to easily go back and forth talking, talking, talking. It seems to go on forever and doesn't seem to have a point. When I talk to my friend Lanny and plan our next racquetball game it sounds like this:

Me: Hey, Lanny, we on for Tuesday?

Lanny: Yeah. Got it.

Me: See you then.

Lanny: Gonna kick your butt, my friend.

Me: Not a chance.

That's it. Clean, clear, quick, and easy.

When I'm talking with a group of my buddies, we often joke, compete, and put each other down in playful ways. We can talk seriously, but there's also a lot of playful competition as we let each other know . . . "I'm top dog." "No, *I'm* top dog!"

I never really understood the difference until I read a book called *Duels and Duets: Why Men and Women Talk So Differently* by John L. Locke, a linguistics professor at City University of New York. Although we often focus on difficulties in communicating between men and women, much less focus has been placed on same-sex communication. Locke has found that the way we talk is not just driven by various cultural norms, but by deep-seated, evolutionary-based, sex differences.

Step 1: Understand that males duel while females duet.

"In birds and mammals, including the other primates," says Locke, "sexually mature males are prone to contend with each other in highly public vocal displays that are aggressive or 'agonistic' in nature."[1] **He describes these male type communications as "duels."**

"In many primate species, sexually mature females have an equally strong disposition to affiliate with other females in more private and intimate circumstances," says Locke.[2] **He describes these female-type communications as "duets."**

When men and women come together they often employ communication styles that are appropriate to their own sex and difficulties often arise. See if you recognize some of these male-type communication traits:

- They interrupt each other.
- They issue commands, threats, or boasts.
- They resist each other's demands.
- They give information.
- They heckle.

— They tell jokes.
— They try to top another's story.
— They insult or denigrate each other.

Likewise, consider these female-type communication traits:

— They agree with other speakers.
— They yield to other speakers.
— They acknowledge points made by other speakers.
— They try and be polite.
— They cooperate.
— They collaborate.
— They empathize.
— They listen.

Of course, as with all male/female differences, these aren't totally separate categories. Many men communicate more toward the female style and many women more toward the male style. We don't want to fall into the trap of thinking that "all men communicate this way" and "all women communicate that way." However, these differences can help us accept our own gender-specific style and help us better understand the other sex.

When my wife and I are having difficulties communicating, she often accuses me of interrupting her and not letting her finish her thought. I accuse her of taking too long to get to the point. Communication that is comfortable to me is either short and to the point, or rapid-fire back and forth that is familiar with my male friends.

Why Is This Important? Men are not aware of "women-only talk" and women are not aware of "men-only talk." I'm never there when my wife is talking to her women friends alone, and she's never in my men's group. As a result we each believe that *real* communication is the type we are familiar with and believe that communication would improve *if only* our partner would learn to listen and speak the way we do. Further, because women are generally more comfortable with verbal communication the female style has come to be viewed as "the right way to communicate." As a result, men often talk less and less and women assume men are not interested in "communicating." Understanding the purpose and value of sex-specific styles can help us appreciate ourselves and our partner more fully. As we'll see, it can also help us appreciate and honor both "male talk" and "female talk."

Step 2: Appreciate that male/female talk has strong evolutionary roots

Our communication styles are not just culture specific and easily modified. They evolved over millions of years to allow males and females to survive and thrive. Male talk and female talk are as different as they are because ancestral men and women competed for the things they needed in two fundamentally different ways.

Imagine that you are living as your ancestors did 500,000 years ago. If you were a man you spent a good deal of time hunting. You walked on animal trails away from the main camp. You had to be quiet, communicating with hand-signals, head and eye movements, and short phrases. If you were a woman you stayed closer to camp, gathered food in an area close to camp, and dealt with noisy children while talking with female friends and relatives.

During thousands of years of our evolutionary history, men and women faced somewhat different challenges that enabled us to survive and reproduce. As we saw in Chapter 2, male genes, bodies, brains, and hormones differ from those of females. It's not surprising that our communication styles and strategies also differ.

Why Is This Important? If we don't understand that differences are part of our evolutionary strategy of survival we tend to devalue the way the other sex communicates. I often hear my women clients complain that their man doesn't communicate with them. What they really mean is that he doesn't talk to her in ways that are familiar to her. When I point out he is communicating all the time, but perhaps with actions rather than words, she can better understand him. Further, when we can appreciate our differences we can recognize that they can be complementary. Locke says that these different strategies can cause men and women to *clash* when they communicate with each other. "The paradox," says Locke, "is that these same modes of speaking make it possible for males and female partners to *mesh* in their lives."[3]

Step 3: Learn to speak the language of the other sex.

Throughout evolutionary history men spent a lot of time with other men, and women spent time with other women. There was an appreciation of the different roles and communication styles of the other. Now we spend more time together in work and in family interaction. As a result, we need to learn to speak the other's language and to be able to understand them when they speak.

For starters, we need to recognize the importance of nonverbal communication. Words aren't the only means of communication and they may, in fact, be the least common. In her studies on gender differences in language use, Deborah Tannen estimates that as much as 90 percent of all human communication is nonverbal, including hand and eye movements, tone of voice, body posture, and so on.[4] Women, as a group, are more fluent verbally, though as is true of all these sex differences, there are exceptions to the rule. In our society we've tended to look at female-type communication as the rule and viewed male-type communication as juvenile or less real. What's more, we often don't recognize that we have a bias, so both women and men will often view female-style communication that is emotional, empathic, cooperative, and polite as "real communication." Male-type communication that is unemotional, analytic, commanding, and joking is seen as "less valuable."

Just as learning a foreign language can help us expand our understanding of other cultures, and allows us to understand and communicate with others, so too can learning the foreign language of the other sex. There are times when female-type talk can be very helpful to both women and men. There are other times when male-type talk is most helpful. If we think of becoming bilingual rather than getting the other to learn our style because it's the right way to communicate, we will all be happier and enjoy a better love life.

Step 4: Don't freak out if your partner says, "I love you, but I'm not *in love* with you."

"I don't love you anymore. I'm not sure I ever did. I'm moving out. The kids will understand. They'll want me to be happy." When Laura Munson heard these words from her husband of twenty years, she did a very strange thing. She didn't cry. She didn't protest. She didn't fight back. She simply decided not to believe him.

In a *New York Times* article titled "Those Aren't Fighting Words, Dear," she offered this visual that many of us have experienced: Child throws a temper tantrum. Tries to hit his mother. But the mother doesn't hit back, lecture, or punish. Instead, she ducks. Then she tries to go about her business as if the tantrum isn't happening. She doesn't "reward" the tantrum. She simply doesn't take the tantrum personally because, after all, it's not about her.

I often see men going through "manopause" express similar sentiments to Laura's husband. (Of course, this can happen to men as well when their wives announce that they've fallen out of love and it's over.) But few people have the insight and courage to do what Laura did. But her experience can help many.

We often recognize the ways children can tell a parent that "I hate you. I hate you. I wish you were dead," and the parent can hear the pain, but not get engaged with the child. It's more difficult when we hear a similar sentiment from an adult, but often it's the right way to handle the angry family member.

Here's what Laura said about her husband. "I'm not saying my husband was throwing a child's tantrum. No. He was in the grip of something else—a profound and far more troubling meltdown that comes not in childhood but in midlife, when we perceive that our personal trajectory is no longer arcing reliably upward as it once did. But I decided to respond the same way I'd responded to my children's tantrums. And I kept responding to it that way. For four months."

I don't love you anymore. I'm not sure I ever did.

"His words came at me like a speeding fist, like a sucker punch, yet somehow in that moment I was able to duck. And once I recovered and composed myself, I managed to say, 'I don't buy it.' Because I didn't."

He drew back in surprise, she remembers. Apparently he'd expected me to burst into tears, to rage at him, to threaten him with a custody battle. Or beg him to change his mind.

So he turned mean. He tried to engage her in fights, but she didn't buy in. It took all her strength not to engage.

She felt overwhelmed with anger and fear. She wanted to fight, to rage, to cry. But she didn't. "Instead," she says, "a shroud of calm enveloped me, and I repeated those words: 'I don't buy it.'" Something miraculous began to happen. As she listened to his pain she decided to give him what he needed, which turned out to be some distance to sort things out. He moved out of the house into a small apartment. As she was able to listen and allow him to work out his own problems, things began to shift in her and how she saw her situation. She wouldn't let herself fall into victimhood.

"I simply had come to understand that I was not at the root of my husband's problem. He was. If he could turn his problem into a marital fight, he could make it about us. I needed to get out of the way so that wouldn't happen."

She simply got on with her life. She planned fun outings for herself and her children. If she wanted him to join them, she offered an invitation, but didn't demand that he respond positively. What happened? Here's what she says:

"And one day, there he was, home from work early, mowing the lawn. A man doesn't mow his lawn if he's going to leave it. Not this man. Then he fixed a door that had been broken for eight years. He made a comment about our front porch needing paint. *Our front porch.* He mentioned needing wood for next winter. Little by little he began talking again about a shared future.[5]

Why Is This Important? I've helped many people do a similar thing to what Laura was able to do on her own. I tell the women: Often when a man believes the "problem is my wife," I remind them, "It's really with life that's the problem." Too many fall into the trap of believing that it takes two people to make a relationship work. If both people aren't willing to commit to the relationship, there's no hope. I've found that isn't true. In an article, "It Takes One to Tango: How You Can Save Your Relationship Even if Your Partner Wants to Leave," I recall the words of the great George Carlin. "It takes two to tango," mused Carlin. "Sounds good, but simple reasoning will reveal that it only takes one to tango. It takes two to tango together, maybe, but one person is certainly capable of tangoing on his own."[6] That's what Laura Munson did. Instead of buying into her husband's midlife problems, she let him work it out himself while she learned to tango on her own. It's an important lesson we can all learn.

Step 5: Listen to the wisdom on marriage from the world's best animal trainers.

We often get caught up in our partner's problems. One of my clients was forever misplacing his keys and yelling at his wife to help him find them. She would leap into action and everyone would be stressed out until the keys were found. That kind of thing would happen to me a lot. Whenever Carlin had a problem, I thought it was my duty to fix it. I would often nag her to get her to do the right thing. Of course, I never considered it nagging. I thought of it as creative problem-solving. Amy Sutherland had a similar problem with keys with her husband.

After seeing Shamu, the killer whale, doing amazing tricks at Sea World in San Diego, journalist Amy Sutherland spent a year following students at Moorpark College's Exotic Animal Training and Management Program, which she describes as "the Harvard University for animal trainers." What she learned changed her life. It taught her to better understand herself, and more important how to improve her relationship with her husband and deepen their love. What she learned was very helpful to me, and I know it will be to you as well.

"The central lesson I learned from exotic animal trainers is that I should reward behavior I like and ignore behavior I don't," says Sutherland.[7] I've found it is one of the most powerful tools in improving our relationship. Instead of trying to correct our partner and get them to shape up, it works much better to ignore behavior we don't like and reward the things that are in the service of our relationship.

"I followed the students to Sea World San Diego, where a dolphin trainer introduced me to least reinforcing syndrome (L.R.S.)," says Sutherland. "When a dolphin does something wrong, the trainer doesn't respond in any way. He stands still for a few beats, careful not to look at the dolphin, and then returns to work. The idea is that any response, positive or negative, fuels a behavior. If a behavior provokes no response, it typically dies away."[8] Sutherland found it worked well with her husband. "It was only a matter of time before he was again tearing around the house searching for his keys, at which point I said nothing and kept at what I was doing. It took a lot of discipline to maintain my calm, but results were immediate and stunning. His temper fell far shy of its usual pitch and then waned like a fast-moving storm. I felt as if I should throw him a mackerel."[9] It may seem strange to use techniques with our mates that animal trainers use, but remember we all want the same things. We want to please those who care about us. Nagging and negativity just bring on more negativity. It's not easy to ignore behavior we don't like and reward what we do like, but it works well. We are all mammals after all.

Step 6: Practicing walking like a man can help men and women.

I'll often hear from women who tell me they can't seem to communicate with their husbands. I suggest they go for a walk together. Here's why. Just as I suggested there were two different ways men and women talk; remember, men duel and women duet—there are two ways men and women engage with each other.

I've found over the years that women tend to be most comfortable communicating *face to face* while men tend to be most comfortable communicating *side by side.* I suspect it may have evolutionary roots that go back to our ancient hunters and gatherers. When men were out hunting they would often sneak up on an animal with each man coming from the side. They would make hand signals to let the other men know their intent. Women would be closer to camp looking at each eye to eye and talking.

Imagine being a man out hunting away from camp. As he stalked the animal he hoped to kill for dinner, he had to worry that there might be other animals stalking him. We've all had the experience of having someone's eyes focused on us. My wife, Carlin, has told me often how it feels to have a man's eyes focused on her. "There are times when it feels frightening. Even if I'm not worried about an assault and rape, a man's eyes can feel predatory."

When men feel eyes focused on them, I think it stimulates body memories of being stalked by a predator. Face-to-face communication, with eyes intently focused, may feel threatening, even if the discussion is mild. Side-by-side communication feels safer, particularly when talking about emotionally charged issues.

"I was amazed at the difference," one of my women clients told me. "I did what you suggested. I asked to go for a walk with my husband when I had some concerns about our son. In the past when I'd sit him down to talk, he would always get angry. Walking side-by-side, he listened attentively and we came up with some new ways to help our son. It never occurred to me that side-by-side communication was something he would find more comfortable, but now I understand. Thank you."

This also works great when talking with teenagers. When I have boys who I see in therapy, I'll often go for a walk and talk. Or we may toss a ball back and forth. Focusing on the ball, rather than sitting closely face-to-face, makes communication easier for many boys. Of course, there are always exceptions. Some boys and men very much enjoy face-to-face communication. One boy I counseled wanted to stop playing and sit down face-to-face so we could "get down to the important stuff."

Another benefit of walking, whether we talk or are silent, is that it seems to be a natural antidepressant. I've often wondered how our hunter–gatherer ancestors dealt with the stresses of life. They didn't have all the same stresses as we have in modern times, but they had to deal with issues of identity, sexuality, bringing home the bacon, and staying healthy. We've always had to deal with the losses and traumas of life.

In his wonderful little book *Walking Your Blues Away: How to Heal the Mind and Create Emotional Well-Being*, Thom Hartmann asks, "How has humankind historically dealt with trauma for the past two hundred thousand years, before the advent of psychotherapy?" His answer is that we walked. As we swing our arms left and right to keep rhythm with our strides, it helps the brain process and heal emotional wounds, without having to talk about them.

In my book *Stress Relief for Men: How to Use the Revolutionary Tools of Energy Healing to Live Well*, I describe walking as the original energy healing tool. You can use it to connect more deeply in your relationship. It's good for healing body, mind, and spirt—as well as the inevitable relationship problems that we all face.

Step 7: Learn how to improve your marriage without talking about it.

When there are relationship problems, it's almost axiomatic that we *know* we should talk about them. All the self-help books tell us that good communication is essential for having a good marriage and good communication, we are told, rests on learning good talking and listening skills. I'm a therapist and marriage and family counselor. I make my living talking to people.

But one of the most important things I've learned being married to my wife, Carlin, for more than thirty-six years is that talking about problems can cause more problems than not talking about them. I know this may sound like heresy to some of you. How can things get better if we don't talk about them? "My husband just ignores our problems," a fifty-two-year-old woman told me. "I've tried everything I can think of to get him to talk to me. I'm coming to the conclusion that he just doesn't care about the relationship."

This has been a conclusion that many women have drawn. I try to help them understand that men care deeply about their relationships and about their mate and family. They just don't believe that talking about problems will improve things. "Women want to talk about the relationship because they are upset and want to feel better," say Patricia Love and Steven Stosny, authors of *How to Improve Your Marriage Without Talking About It*. "Men *don't* want to talk because talking *won't* make them feel better. In fact it will make them feel worse."[10]

I learned this lesson from my wife. As is true of about 10 percent of the population, I have the more female-type brain. I love to talk. My wife has a more male-type brain. She is less comfortable with talking and expressing strong emotions, particularly anger.

People with male-type brains often become "flooded" when they talk about emotion-laden concerns and talking about the relationship is always emotion laden. That's why men will say the five words they dread the most are "Honey, we need to talk." What often happens is that the more one person wants to talk about an issue, the more fearful the other person becomes. As a result they become more and more distant. The person who wants to talk despairs at getting more deeply connected, and the person who resists talking feels alternately attacked and ignored.

Robert, one of my clients, talked about how it felt interacting with his wife. "I feel like she is always pecking at me. It's like a blue jay, peck, peck, pecking on my head. It feels like I can't do anything right, that nothing I do ever pleases her." His wife, Sarah, is equally frustrated. "If I don't keep at him, he just ignores our problems. I'm so afraid that we're drifting apart and if I don't get through to him our marriage is going to go under."

Most all couples have had these kinds of experiences. One person says or does something that triggers a response from the other partner. The response then triggers a response, and couples often get caught in a downward spiral that keeps them locked into negativity and can undermine their relationships. Here are some things I've learned that can help couples break out of these cycles.

- Before you react, pause and take a deep breath. Notice the sensations coming from your body. Resist the urge to respond. When things aren't going right in our relationships we all get scared. When we act from fear, rather than love, we usually make the problem worse.

- When you do respond, offer "I" messages, rather than "You" messages. "*I* felt hurt when you said that," rather than "*You* are always criticizing me."

- Remember, the stresses of life can make us all more reactive. Remind yourself that this is your friend and lover, not your enemy. Be caring, even when you feel angry or hurt.

- Find ways to connect without talking. Too often we think that "talking things out" is the only way to solve problems. Walking in nature, giving each other a massage, or just looking into each other's eyes can create bonds of love.

- When you talk to your partner and even when you're talking in your own mind, focus on the positive. Say what you like, not what you don't like. Say what you want, not what you don't want.

Why Is This Important? When we are having problems, usually one partner, more than the other, may want to talk their way out of it. But talking can cause more problems than it solves. Remember, we are all animals and the best animal trainers have learned many techniques that work without words. I'm not suggesting that we should never talk out our problems but that there are other ways to connect without words. Sometimes words can help, but too often they get in the way. I've had to learn to talk less and find ways of communication that worked best with Carlin. I trust you'll find your own ways to live and love more fully and deeply.

Seven

Midlife Depression: Why Men Act Out and Women Act In

I 've been running from depression my whole life. My midlife father tried to take his own life when I was five years old. I grew up wondering what happened to my father and if it would happen to me. My mother was terrified that I'd follow in my father's footsteps, and because he was a creative artist and writer, my mother associated creativity and craziness. I thought keeping my feelings under control and pursuing a business career would keep me safe. When my business became a creative endeavor, I felt I had to run even faster to keep depression at bay.

As I got older I couldn't seem to run as fast, and I struggled with depression and the same manic-depressive (bipolar) illness that nearly killed my father. My struggle was mostly internal. I maintained a good façade and appeared to be super-competent. I went to graduate school and became a therapist, only partly subconsciously, in order to protect myself from going crazy. I thought if I learned about depression and other "mental illnesses" somehow they would pass me by.

That all changed when my wife, Carlin, and I were invited to a weekend family gathering. Our son had entered treatment to deal with his drug problems, and family members were invited to learn about recovery and support their loved ones. As part of the weekend experience, all the family members were given a standard depression questionnaire. The reason given was that often family members who have relatives with addiction problems suffer from depression at higher rates than the general population.

We each took the questionnaire and my wife scored "high," indicating that she was suffering from depression. I scored "low" indicating that I was not. When we returned home Carlin went to see a psychiatrist and her diagnosis was confirmed. She began taking medications and things began to improve greatly in her life and in mine. She worried less and was much less preoccupied with "everything that could possibly go wrong." Her constant ruminations declined, and she was much more joyful in her outlook on life.

When things improved for Carlin she had a clearer picture of life. She told me she thought I might be depressed. I told her she was wrong and became defensive. When she persisted I became irritable and angry. "I'm a psychotherapist," I told her. "Don't you think I'd know if I was depressed?" She countered, "Well, you didn't recognize that *I* was depressed," she pointed out. She had a point.

But I reminded her that I had scored low on the depression questionnaire. That was my trump card, proving I wasn't depressed. She backed off, but over the next few months my unhappiness increased and my irritability was evident. Of course I could justify my anger and irritability. "Who wouldn't be angry," I would say, "if you had to put up with what I had to put up with?" I'd proceed to blame all the people in my life who seemingly were going out of their way to get on my last nerve.

Finally, with her care and support I agreed to see the doctor who had evaluated her for depression. I didn't like him much. He was somewhat aloof, but after an hour interview he concluded,

"We could probably debate about whether you're bipolar I or bipolar II, but you definitely have it and your life would likely improve if you were treated." I thanked him and left, thinking somewhat crazily, "What does he know?"

When I got home Carlin wanted to know what he said. I told her, but emphasized that I wasn't convinced and wanted to get a second opinion. She got a bit heated. "You want a second opinion? Well, here it is. You've got a problem. Get some help." Once again she backed off. She knew that pushing me further would just create more resistance.

I asked around and found another psychiatrist. This one was a woman whom I liked much better. She seemed open, honest, and willing to listen. I recounted my history and my symptoms and waited for her to tell me I was fine, just too much stress in my life. But that's not what she said. "We could probably debate about whether you're bipolar I or bipolar II, but you definitely have it." The words were exactly what the other doctor had told me.

This time I listened. I began taking medications. I went back weekly for psychotherapy. I kept a log of my moods and thoughts. I read everything I could on depression, manic depression (which now is usually called bipolar illness), and how men and women are diagnosed. I resonated with the words of Kay Redfield Jamison, PhD, one of the experts in the field of psychiatry and mood disorders, and herself someone who suffered from bipolar illness. In her book *An Unquiet Mind: Memoir of Moods and Madness*, she says: "You're irritable and paranoid and humorless and lifeless and critical and demanding, and no reassurance is ever enough. You're frightened, and you're frightening, and 'you're not at all like yourself but will be soon,' but you know you won't."[1]

Why Is This Important? Jamison's memoir opened my heart, my mind, and my soul. By sharing her experiences she demonstrated that even a highly regarded expert could suffer from depression. Her courage to share her story helped ease the shame I felt about my father's "craziness" and my own. In a few words she captured what life was like for me and for Carlin. I was irritable and felt others were the cause of my problems. Deep inside, I was terribly frightened, but I came across with anger and frightened others, though I was always surprised that my wife said she was afraid of me. I never hit her, but my eyes were cold. She would tell me, "You get those beady eyes and it chills me to the bone." I kept thinking, "I'll snap out of it. I don't need help. I can do it myself," but I finally accepted that I was human like everyone else and I could either "do it myself" and continue to hurt my wife and stay stuck, or I could get the help I needed.

I went on to spend the next few years doing research that culminated in two books, the first a popular book for everyone, *The Irritable Male Syndrome: Understanding and Managing the 4 Key Causes of Depression and Aggression*. The second book is for professionals, based on my research to develop a better diagnostic tool for men, *Male vs. Female Depression: Why Men Act Out and Women Act In*. Here's what I've learned over the years that you'll find helpful.

Step 1: Recognize that midlife is a real downer.

We can suffer from depression at any time in the life cycle, but midlife is a particularly difficult period. In fact, research shows that "midlife is a real downer." Using data on 2 million people, from eighty nations, researchers from the University of Warwick and Dartmouth College in the United States have found an extraordinarily consistent international pattern in depression and happiness levels that leaves us most miserable in middle age. Researchers discovered that "for both men and women, the probability of depression peaks around 44 years of age."[2]

Charting happiness shows a U-shaped curve, with relative highs at the beginning of life (the joys of youth) and post-midlife (the golden years), but with a very clear low period during middle age. The research was aimed at identifying unhappiness patterns, but it was not structured to pinpoint causes, leaving researchers to hypothesize why midlife is so darn tough. One of theories is that middle age begins with the realization that one won't achieve all of one's aspirations and then ends after "seeing their fellow middle-aged peers begin to die," therefore kicking off a period where they value their own remaining years and embrace life once more. If true, this would explain why people who express gratitude and people who are goal oriented generally record higher happiness levels.

Another contributing cause could be the large number of life changes that can happen during this period. In the span of just a decade individuals can experience empty nest, taking care of our parents and losing them as they die, marital stress and divorce, unemployment and job changes, financial pressure, menopause/ andropause, and possibly serious illness. This is also the time that looking in the mirror can highlight the effects that the passage of time has had on our appearance. We might have the psychological strength to handle one or two of these, but the cumulative effect of too many of them might simply be too much.

Why Is This Important? When we're unhappy for long periods of time, we want to understand why. We sometimes blame ourselves or our partner. This research reminds us that this is a very difficult time of life and doesn't mean that there's something wrong with us, with our partner, or with the relationship. Although there are always things we can do to improve how we feel at any age, when we feel stuck it helps to know that things will likely get better with time.

Across almost all eighty countries in the study, they found that if you make it to age seventy and are still physically fit, you are on average as "happy and mentally healthy as a twenty-year-old."[3] Carlin and I are both in our seventies now, and I can say that it's true. Of course if you're in pain and you're fifty it may not help to hear "Hang in there until you're seventy and you'll feel better." But it can help to recognize, even in the middle of your down period, there's nothing wrong with you or your mate. You're just at the bottom of the "U," and it will be uphill from here.

Step 2: Understand that depression manifests differently in women than in men.

One difference is that women hit bottom at an earlier age than men. The researchers found that in the United States women are most unhappy around age forty, whereas men hit bottom, on average at age fifty. Women who recognize their depression and get help may be ahead of men who may take longer to recognize and deal with their irritability and low moods.

Further, the symptoms that men experience may be different from those of women. For years the worldwide literature indicated that women experience depression at twice the rate of men. But my experience led me to believe that men may experience depression as often as women, but express it differently. In my book *The Irritable Male Syndrome: Understanding and Recognizing the 4 Key Causes of Depression and Aggression,* I say, "I think male depression is often masked. Those of us who live with depression wear a mask that hides what we are really feeling from others and even from ourselves. People don't know we are depressed because what they see doesn't look like the kind of depression they are familiar with. We also mask our depression with other things like anger, alcohol, and chronic withdrawal."[4] I think of the differences this way: Just as there are two life forces in the natural world, the outer-directed *dynamic* and the inner directed *magnetic,* I believe there are *dynamic depressions,* which are expressed by "acting out" our inner turmoil, and *magnetic depressions*, which are expressed by "acting in" our pain. Men are more likely to experience dynamic depressions, and women are more likely to experience magnetic depressions.

Women often express their depression by blaming themselves. Men often express their depression by blaming others—their wives, bosses, the economy, the government—anyone or anything *but* themselves.

Why Is This Important? For too long we've assumed that depression manifests itself the same in women and men. As a result, a woman may recognize she has a problem and get help, whereas a man insists that "I'm not depressed, damn it!" Once we have a better understanding of the ways depression can manifest, we can better know ourselves and appreciate what our partner is dealing with. When both Carlin and I got help with our depression, we felt a lot better about our lives and our relationship improved greatly.

Step 3: Realize that we often miss depression in males.

In a revealing experiment, J. Douglas Bremner, MD, gathered a group of former depression patients. With their permission, he gave them a beverage that was spiked with an amino acid that blocks the brain's ability to absorb serotonin (the brain neurotransmitter that is linked to a positive mood). Typical of the males was John, a middle-aged businessman who had fully recovered from a bout of depression, thanks to a combination of psychotherapy and Prozac. Within minutes of drinking the brew, however, "He wanted to escape to a bar across the street," recalls Dr. Bremner. **"He didn't express sadness . . . he didn't really express anything. He just wanted to go to Larry's Lounge."**

Contrast John's response with that of female subjects like Sue, a mother of two in her mid-thirties. After taking the cocktail,

"She began to cry and express her sadness over the loss of her father two years ago," recalls Dr. Bremner. "She was overwhelmed by her emotions."[5] Marianne J. Legato, MD, FACP, an expert on gender and depression, found "when their serotonin levels drop, women tend to withdraw and become anxious and reclusive. Men, on the other hand, respond to low serotonin levels with aggressive behavior."

Why Is This Important? Depressed women often appear sad, and as a result get more understanding and support from others. Depressed men often appear to be mad, and as a result people want to get away from them. Understanding that men's irritability and anger is often a call for help can save relationships and save lives.

Step 4: Ask yourself why women seek help while men die.

"Women seek help. Men die."

This conclusion was drawn from a study of suicide and found that 75 percent of those who sought professional help in an institution for suicide prevention were female. Conversely, 75 percent of those who committed suicide in the same year were male. Because depression is a significant risk factor for suicide and men receive less treatment for depression than do women, it is vitally important that we have a better understanding of the way depression manifests itself in males.

When we look at suicide statistics for men and women, we see some interesting differences:

- At every age the suicide rate is higher for males than for females.
- Both male and female suicide rates go up between the ages of thirty-five and fifty-five.
- Between ages sixty-five and seventy-four males commit suicide at six times the rate of females.

- Between seventy-five and eighty-four, the rate jumps to seven times higher for males than females.
- And over eighty-five, the fastest-growing demographic in the country, the suicide rate for males is nearly 18 times higher than for females.[6]

Clearly, we need to be paying more attention to male depression as men enter midlife, reach retirement age, and as they get older.

Step 5: Pay attention to male loneliness as we age.

At every age the suicide rate is higher for males than for females. And over eighty-five, the fastest-growing demographic in the country, the suicide rate for males is 18 times higher than for females. Clearly, we need to be paying more attention to male depression at midlife and after. The male/female ratio is greatest as men retire and age: 6.3 times higher for men than for women sixty-five to seventy-four, 7 times higher for men than for women seventy-five to eighty-four, and 17.5 times higher for men than for women eighty-five-plus. I never realized how lonely life could be until I got divorced. My wife got custody of the kids, and I didn't realize how much I would miss seeing them every day until I became the "noncustodial parent." I soon realized that most of *our* friends were actually *her* friends. The friends I had before we got married had mostly drifted away, and I hadn't made new ones. My wife had become the social secretary, and I counted on her to plan the parties and keep us connected with our family, friends, and neighbors.

It was my feelings of loneliness that helped me reach out to men and start a men's group. We've been meeting now for thirty-six years, and the first man died recently. There are now six of us still going. Both Carlin and I credit the men's group as being instrumental in helping me deal with depression and the loneliness that is often at its core.

Over the years I've learned the benefits of such things as good nutrition and exercise to helping us live more healthy lives. I've only recently learned about the benefits of social connection. In their book *Loneliness: Human Nature and the Need for Social Connection,* researchers John Cacioppo and William Patrick say that **"social isolation is on a par with high blood pressure, obesity, lack of exercise, or smoking as a risk factor for illness and early death."**[7]

Studies also demonstrate that men, as a group, have fewer social connections than women. In workshops over the years, I have asked the women in the audience, "How many of you have a number of close friends that you talk to about important things in your life and who you turn to when you are hurting physically or emotionally?" Most all the women raise their hands. When I ask the same question of men, very few raise their hands. Most women have many close friends and confidants among their relatives and friends. For most men, their only real friend may be their spouse, and if there's trouble in the relationship they are totally alone.

I learned that, like me, men often have fewer and fewer close friends as we get older. This may contribute to the fact that the suicide rate for men goes up dramatically as we age. Thomas Joiner, PhD, author of *Lonely at the Top: The High Cost of Men's Success,* says, "Men's main problem is not self-loathing, stupidity, greed, or any of the legions of other things they're accused of. **The problem, instead is loneliness."**[8] Dr. Joiner notes that with age, men gradually lose contact with friends and family. "And here's the important part," he tells us, "they don't replenish them."[9] Instead of maintaining our friendships and developing new ones when old friends slip away, we look for Band-Aid solutions to cover our loneliness. Some of us become more workaholic; others escape into alcohol or drugs. Some have extramarital affairs. These pseudo-solutions only serve to increase our loneliness.

Most of us realize that it's never too late to change our diet or improve our exercise regimen. Likewise, it's never too late for us to admit we're lonely, reach out to others, improve our relationships, and make new friends. It may be the best health advice we'll ever receive. The alternative isn't pleasant. A postmortem report on a suicide decedent, a man in his sixties, read, "He did not have friends. . . . He did not feel comfortable with other men . . . he did not trust doctors and would not seek help even though he was aware that he needed help."[10] Think about your friends. Who do you know that you feel comfortable sharing your deepest feelings, your hopes and fears? Reflect on the friends you have had who may have fallen away. Is it time to reconnect with some of those friends? Is it time to make new friends?

Step 6: Know that it's important to name our depression, not label it.

Even though both Carlin and I went to a doctor and were prescribed medications that were helpful, we don't consider depression a "mental illness." Being diagnosed as having one of the illnesses described in the official *Diagnostic and Statistical Manual of Mental Disorders* (DSM) helped us get insurance reimbursement for our treatment, but I haven't found it helpful to think of myself, or my wife, as "mentally ill."

There may be some benefits to being labelled as "depressed," but there are also some drawbacks. I've found being labelled by others doesn't capture the full extent of my own experience or empower me to find real, lasting solutions. Carlin wrote a wonderful book called *Love it, Don't Label It: A Practical Guide for Using Spiritual Principles in Everyday Life.* She says, "When we assign *a label* to someone or something we often related to the label and not to the person or thing we have labeled."[11] To illustrate, she had twelve pictures taken of herself, each one in a different setting, with a different look. In one she looked like a cheerleader, in another like a biker babe. One picture had her in tight pants in front of the local bar. She had all the appearances of a hooker. In another picture she looked old and depressed, with a bottle of vodka in front of her. Each one reminds us how we often label others and even ourselves, usually in ways that are less than positive.

Sometimes it's important to give a *name* to who we are or what we have. There was a time I found it empowering to name myself manic-depressive. It captured the wild swings in mood I often experienced. The name empowered me and I didn't feel it was who I was. It didn't lock me into a diagnosis. The official manual had me labeled as bipolar. I still like the old name. It works for me, and when it doesn't I'll let it go. I encourage you to do the same. If naming what you have as *depression* or what-ever, take it, own it, love it. Don't label yourself, and don't label your partner.

I like the way Andrew Solomon, author of *The Noonday Demon: An Atlas of Depression*, describes his experience: "Depression is a flaw in love. To be creatures who love, we must be creatures who can despair at what we lose, and depression is the mechanism of that despair."[12] From this point of view, depression is not an illness, but an indicator that we are losing important people or experiences of love and support.

Step 7: Accept that depression is a wake-up call for what we are losing of our world.

We usually focus on depression as an individual problem, but I suggest that it is really a social problem. Depression is on the rise worldwide, and according to the World Health Organization by

2030 depression will the leading cause of disease burden in the world. Whether we are consciously aware of it or not, we are losing the very things we need as a species to survive.

The world's population is now well in excess of 7 billion and growing. It's difficult to grasp population growth, but this helped me get a better feel for the problem. We are adding 200,000 more people to the planet every day, or 140 every minute. That equates to 70 million more people every year, about the same as the combined population of California, Texas, and Washington. Think about that for a minute (and, as you do, another 140 people have been added). All those people want what you want; clean air, water, a home, food, and so on. But the resources on the planet are limited. Whether we are aware of it, we all feel the pressure as we compete for the scare resources on a finite planet.

Reliable reports on the planet's health, such as the United Nations' Global Environment Outlook, have found water, land, plants, animals, and fish stocks are all "in inexorable decline." The UN warns bluntly that world population "has reached a stage where the amount of resources needed to sustain it exceeds what is available."[13] The annual population increase of more than 70 million equates to a city for 1.5 million people having to be built, somewhere, every week—with, inevitably, ever more greenhouse gas emissions and the continuing destruction of forests and wetlands, with their multiple habitats for the web of life on which all species depend.

Whether we just give up or try to do something constructive, we all feel the stress. If we're not depressed to some degree, we're in denial. There are a number of organizations that I think are really making a difference in the world. One program I'm involved with is the Ecology Action, Grow Biointensive Farming Movement (*www.growbiointensive.org*), which is teaching people worldwide how to farm in a way that nurtures healthy soil fertility, produces high yields, conserves resources, and can be used successfully by almost everyone. Another is the Post Carbon Institute (*www.postcarbon.org*), which is leading the transition to a more resilient, equitable, and sustainable world by providing individuals and communities with the resources needed to understand and respond to the interrelated economic, energy, and ecological crises of the twenty-first century.

I believe that couples can work together to accept that much of the depression we all feel comes from recognizing the reality of what our children, grandchildren, and future generations will be facing. It may be overwhelming to deal with alone, but couples can join with others to make a difference for all the children of the world. We are certainly facing difficult times ahead. Carlin and I remind ourselves that we're all going to die sometime. While we're here, we are doing our best to experience the joy of living on this wonderful planet. We are also doing what we can to keep our planet alive and well for future generations.

Eight

Navigating the Change of Life: New Understanding for Men and Women

*M*y search to understand andropause began in the early 1990s and was both personal and professional. Personally, I was nearing the age of fifty and my wife was telling me something was wrong. "You're hormonal," she told me. "It's like you're going through menopause or something." At first I laughed at the idea. Like most people I didn't believe men went through a "change of life" that was similar to what women experienced.

Professionally, my colleague Gail Sheehy, author of *Passages* and *Menopause: The Silent Passage,* wrote an article in 1993. "If menopause is the silent passage," said Sheehy, " 'male menopause' is the unspeakable passage. It is fraught with secrecy, shame, and denial. It is much more fundamental than the ending of the fertile period of a woman's life, because it strikes at the core of what it is to be a man."[1] Though the "change of life" impacts both men and women, much more attention has been placed on understanding what women go through during the "menopause" passage. Although there has been an increased understanding of the "male change of life" (aka andropause, male menopause, or manopause), we are still way behind in our knowledge and understanding. Because both men and women will benefit from knowing more, I'm focusing this chapter more on the man's change of life than on the woman's, although both are equally important.

As a clinician and writer who works with men and their families, I decided I better learn about male menopause. I conducted clinical research with men and women throughout the world that resulted in a series of books, *Male Menopause, Surviving Male Menopause*, and *The Irritable Male Syndrome*, which reported our findings.

I found that both men and women had difficulty talking seriously about "the change of life." Many men think that anything with "pause" in the title is something "feminine" and they best run the other way, whether we're talking about *manopause, andropause*, or *male menopause*. But even women who break the silence often make jokes when talking about menopause.

"I call the Change of Life 'Orchids,'" says Lisa Jey Davis, author of *Getting Over Your Ovaries: How to Make 'The Change of Life' Your Bitch*, "because menopause is such an ugly word. It's got men in it for goddsakes."[2]

There's still a great deal we are learning about male menopause. Jonathan V. Wright, MD, and Lane Lenard, PhD, authors of *Maximize Your Vitality and Potency*, say, "Although the idea has been around in one form or another for thousands of years, until *very* recently the existence of a hormonally driven male menopause analogous to that experienced by women was widely denied by the forces that rule mainstream medicine."[3]

When I first started doing research for *Male Menopause* there was very little written in the United States. Most of the studies had been going on in other countries. After it was published it was translated into fifteen foreign languages, and I developed a worldwide following. It gained popularity in the United States when I answered a letter I had read in *Dear Abby*.

"Dear Abby:

I am a 50-year-old man who has been married for 22 years. My wife and I have two wonderful teen-aged children. About six months ago, my wife's niece (I'll call her Rene), whom I had never met, came from another country to live with us so she could go to college in the United States. She is in her early 20s."

As I read Abigail Van Buren's (Dear Abby) column in my local newspaper, I shook my head and thought, "Here's another family headed for trouble."

The letter went on: "For the first few months everything was fine. Now I find myself thinking about Rene all the time. I think I'm in love with her. I travel quite a bit because of my job and every time I come home it's torture. I have to act as if nothing is going on in my mind. No one knows the way I feel. If I tell my wife, she'll be crushed and it will be the end of our marriage. If I tell Rene—who has done nothing wrong and loves my wife like a mother—she may want to return to her country without finishing her studies.

"I have always tried to do the right thing. I never thought at this age I'd be feeling this way. I don't want to ruin anyone's life, including my own. What should I do?"

Desperate in Delaware

Abby's response was direct and clear.

"Dear Desperate:

Although it's common for older men to fantasize about younger women, the consequences of your fantasy could irreparably damage at least five lives. Talking this out with someone you trust would be helpful. I recommend a professional therapist, who can help you assess the consequences of acting out this fantasy."[4] Though Abby's advice was good, I felt it didn't go far enough. There are deeper issues that need to be addressed. What is really going on in the lives of millions of midlife men? How can we help our teenage children deal with their physical, hormonal, sexual, and emotional lives when we are so confused about our own? How can we help families get through this difficult time of life without splitting apart? Based on my own research that resulted in the publication of my book *Male Menopause,* I sent a response to Dear Abby with a summary of what I had learned from my research.

I was pleasantly surprised that my letter ran under a headline for her column that appeared in newspapers all over the country: SYMPTOMS OF MALE MENOPAUSE ARE REAL.

I'll share with you what I had learned writing my books, what I shared with the Dear Abby readers, and new information that I have developed from recent research and clinical practice.

Step 1: Understand the basics of the "male change of life."

When I first began doing research for my first book on the "male change of life," *Male Menopause,* I was skeptical. I understood that women experienced real changes during this period of life. Hormone levels dropped dramatically, and their ability to repro-duce ended. I assumed that whatever men might go through it was nothing like that of women. However, my own research, which has now been backed up by the work of many others, con-vinced me that there are many similarities between what men and women experience.

Here are some of the basics you should know about the male change of life, which I'll call *manopause* from here on out:

- Manopause begins with hormonal, physiological, and chemical changes that occur in all men generally between the ages of forty and fifty-five, though it can occur as early as thirty-five or as late as sixty-five.
- These changes affect all aspects of a man's life. Manopause is, thus, a multidimensional change of life that includes hormonal, physical,

psychological, interpersonal, sexual, social, and spiritual dimensions.

— Just as both males and females go through puberty when hormones come on line, both males and females experience a "change of life" when hormones decline and we go through other major life changes. Issues of sexual desire, identity, dependence, and independence become important.

— The purpose of manopause is to signal the end of the first part of a man's life and prepare him for the second half. Rather than the beginning of the end as many fear, it is actually the passage to the most powerful, productive, and purposeful time of a man's life.

— **Emotional symptoms** may include restlessness, irritability, indecisiveness, and worry.

— **Physical symptoms** may include fatigue, weight gain, sleep disturbances, and memory loss.

— **Sexual symptoms** may include loss of libido, erectile dysfunction, fear of failure, and desire to prove they can still perform sexually.

— There seem to be two common approaches for addressing manopause. One group of clinicians believes the male change of life is a myth and men should accept the changes as a natural part of aging. The other group believes that manopause is real and is synonymous with "low testosterone." The treatment of choice, in this view, is simply to replace testosterone that declines as we age.

— I take a third approach that recognizes that manopause is real, but is more complex that merely treating "Low-T." I offer a variety of possible interventions including special diet, exercise, weight loss (fat cells around the belly convert testosterone to estrogen), deceasing alcohol consumption (too much alcohol lowers testosterone), lowering stress levels and improving sleep (both help keep your testosterone levels up), and bio-identical testosterone replacement for men whose testosterone levels are too low.

Step 2: Get to know testosterone.

Long before testosterone was discovered, the life-changing effects of low testosterone were well known. Microbiologist and author Paul De Kruif says, "From the beginning of human record, priests, saints, medicine men, farmers and sultans had been demonstrating how clear-cut, sure and simple it was to take the vigor of animals and men away. How? By removing their testicles."[5] But men need not lose their testicles to find their virility and vitality waning as their testosterone declines.

There's no question that men's testosterone or "T" levels are at their peak in their twenties and slowly decline thereafter. But on many other issues related to testosterone it is not so easy to separate fact from fiction. For instance, most people don't know these facts:

- Although we think of testosterone as the quintessential male hormone, both women and men produce testosterone and both men and women produce the "female" hormone estrogen.
- Normal testosterone ranges in men vary between 300 and 1,100 ng/dl. In women, levels vary between 15 and 70 ng/dl.
- There are 60 million men in the United States between the ages of thirty-five and sixty-five who are concerned about their testosterone levels.

Step 3: Recognize that too little testosterone is as bad as too much

Many of us know that too much testosterone is bad for us. We hear about professional athletes and bodybuilders who use testosterone-like steroid hormones to bulk up their bodies and increase strength and stamina. Too much can cause problems. According to Charles Patrick Davis, MD, PhD, people who overdo use can "develop high blood pressure, liver disease, shrinkage of testicles, and increased aggression."[6]

When I was researching my book *The Irritable Male Syndrome: Understanding and Managing the 4 Key Causes of Depression and Aggression*, I found that too little testosterone was much more common than too much. I got on to this when I found that one of the most common symptoms of manopause was irritability. It was right up there with erectile dysfunction and loss of libido with 80–90 percent of men experiencing these symptoms during manopause.

I learned about research that was going on in Scotland by Gerald A. Lincoln, PhD. Interestingly, his team was trying to develop a male birth-control pill. They tried lowering the testosterone levels of rams. It didn't stop conception, but he found that the rams became irritable and angry, biting their cages and anyone who got too close. They found a similar irritable response to lowering testosterone in other mammals. When I contacted him, he told me he thought low testosterone contributed to what he called "the irritable male syndrome" in all male mammals, but he had no data on humans. I said I had found the same thing in men. I decided to write a book, and he allowed me to use his term "irritable male syndrome."

Why Is This Important? There are a lot of myths about testosterone. Some see it as the fountain of youth that can keep us forever young and cure all our ills. Others see it as "the hormone from hell," making men aggressive and violent, with uncontrollable sexual desires. The truth is that testosterone is a natural part of our body's communication system and needs to be kept up so we maintain our health, power, passion, and purpose at midlife and beyond.

Step 4: Accept that some men have naturally lower T levels and others have naturally high T levels.

There is quite a large range of what a normal level of testosterone should be. As I said earlier, our peak levels, which we reach in our twenties, may range between 300 and 1,100 ng/dl. Because T levels decrease with age, there is some controversy about what a healthy level should be. Except in a minority of cases, most of the problems people have are when their T levels get too low. However, within the healthy range, some people are naturally lower in testosterone than others. We live in a culture where we often view "more as better," but this isn't the case with testosterone.

James McBride Dabbs, PhD, one of the leading researchers in the field, is the author of *Heroes, Rogues, and Lovers: Testosterone and Behavior*. In his research Dr. Dabbs found that there are actually two kinds of people who differ in their normal levels of testosterone. "Frank Sinatra sang, 'I did it my way,' and the Beatles sang 'I get by with a little help from my friends,'" Dr. Dabbs reminds us. "These are the ways in which high- and low-testosterone people approach the world. Sinatra's song is the self-congratulatory, high testosterone way. They are opposing strategies, one based on dominance and the other on cooperation."[7] When I think of higher T and lower T, I often think of the Rolling Stones and the Beatles. They started at about the same time, dominated the music world, and will leave a lasting legacy. In contrasting the two groups, writer Tom Wolfe said, "The Beatles Want to Hold Your Hand. But The Stones Want to Burn Your Town." Can you guess which one might be the higher-T group?

Dr. Dabbs found a number of interesting differences between higher-T and lower-T people. "High-testosterone people seem to be unhappy when they are alone and happy when they are with people. . . . Low-testosterone people, on the other hand, seem to be less compulsively social."[8] We can see this in the testosterone levels of various professions. Dabbs and his team measured the testosterone levels of physicians, firemen, football players, salesmen, professors, ministers, and actors. He found that ministers, as a group, had the lowest testosterone levels, actors the highest, and the other groups in between.

My father was an actor and in the early years of his career he was a very ambitious, highly sexual, very social, and often irritable. "Actors want to be stars," Dr. Dabbs says, "while ministers want to help." I chose not to follow in my father's footsteps and went into the helping professions. (I must say, though, that when I toured for my book and did my first major TV show, I felt the rush of being on stage.)

Even though high-T people are very social, they can also be more irritable and confrontational. "On the average, high-testosterone individuals are tougher, and low testosterone individuals are friendlier," says Dr. Dabbs.[9]

This difference may have evolutionary advantages in how we reproduce and raise children. Higher testosterone may be important in securing a mate, but lower testosterone may be better for being a good parent and caregiver. Dr. Dabbs, in fact, found that married men are lower in testosterone than single men and that testosterone levels drop when men get married and go up when they get divorced. He also found that men have higher levels of prolactin and lower levels of testosterone immediately after they become fathers. "Perhaps these hormonal changes set them up for the gentler activities of parenthood," Dr. Dabbs concludes.[10] "Know thyself," is a central tenet of philosophers going back as far as Socrates. Getting to know ourselves is an important part of our life's journey. "He who knows others is learned," said Lao-Tzu. "He who knows himself is wise." Getting to know about your own, unique, levels of testosterone surely is an important part of our self-knowledge.

Why Is This Important? In our more-is-better society, too many men want their testosterone levels raised no matter what the levels are. But like all else in life, balance is important. There are times when we want our testosterone to be higher. If we're fighting adversity and winning is important, having a high T level is a good thing. When we're single and courting, higher T gives us an edge. But when we're taking care of our baby girl or enjoying deep talks and intimacy with our partner, we'd like our T levels to be at the lower end of normal. As we get older and T levels drop, there is value in our being less aggressive and more collaborative, less *me* centered and more *we* centered, less concerned about winning and more concerned about helping others to succeed.

Step 5: Find out if your testosterone levels are too low for health and well-being.

We can take some comfort in recognizing that there is a range of healthy testosterone levels and being a lower-T man (who likes the Beatles) is just as good as being a higher-T man (who likes the Rolling Stones). There may be times in our lives when being lower T is better than being higher T or vice versa.

How do you know if your testosterone levels are too low? There are two basic ways we determine that. First, we look at any symptoms you may have indicating you are on the low end. Here are the common symptoms I look at with clients who come to see me. Check off each of the symptoms you experience or notice.

1. Reduced libido or sex drive
2. Difficulty obtaining or maintaining an erection

3. Irritability or grumpiness
4. Fatigue or loss of vitality
5. Aches, pains, or stiffness
6. Forgetfulness or difficulty concentrating
7. Feeling lonely, unattractive, or unloved
8. Impaired relationship with partner
9. Flushing, night sweats
10. Increased sexual dissatisfaction with self or partner

If your symptoms give cause for concern, I'd have you get your testosterone levels, and often other hormone levels, checked. Your doctor can order the tests. One of the best labs I've found is ZRT Laboratory in Oregon. If you don't have a doctor who understands hormonal health, ZRT can help you find a knowledgeable doctor in your area. This innovative lab is headed by Dr. David Zava, one of the leading experts in the field of hormonal health. Whether you get lab tests with them or not, you can visit their site to learn a great deal about hormones and health.

Once your lab results are back, I review your symptoms, your test results, and talk with you about your life and what your needs are at this stage of life. Then we come up with a plan to make things better. Whether you work with me or someone else, it's important to have a partner who looks at you as a whole person and is knowledgeable about all aspects of your health, including hormonal, physical, psychological, interpersonal, sexual, economic, and spiritual.

Step 6: Deal with the challenges of the manopause passage.

It would make life a lot easier if the only thing going on during manopause was a drop in testosterone. But there is a lot more we have to know. Testosterone isn't the only important hormone. As I described in Chapter 2, there are a number of other hormones that also change over time. As a result, hormonal balance is important. For instance, many men may have normal testoster-one levels, but their estrogen levels are elevated.

When I think about the challenges we face during this change of life, I include all of the following:

- Hormone levels are dropping.
- Sexual vigor is diminishing.
- Erections are less frequent and less firm.
- The beautiful image we had of our partner when we first fell in love is replaced by one who looks much older and less attractive to us.
- Our own image of youthful vigor and physical prow-ess has changed, and we see ourselves through the negative lens of "getting old."
- Children are leaving home.
- We may long to follow them, but feel trapped in a life we're not sure we chose.
- Parents are getting sick and dying.
- Job horizons are narrowing.
- Job security is gone.
- Retirement seems less and less possible.
- Friends are having their first heart attacks and cancer scares.
- Hopes and dreams are fading away.

Too many of us accept these negative experiences as we reach this time of life. But that has less to do with the inevitabilities of aging as much as it has to do with our cultural beliefs about aging. If we believe getting older goes with physical, emotional, and sexual decline, that's what we'll expect in our lives. On the other hand, if we expect these years to be full of adventure, new opportunities, deepening love, and offering greater gifts to our communities, that is what we will have. Here are a few things I did after I passed age sixty:

I returned to graduate school and got a PhD in
International Health.

— I ran a marathon (26.2 miles), which was one of the
highlights of my life.

— I was with my wife's mother when she died and felt I
had looked into the face of God.

— I've written four new books, including my first children's book, and continue to write.

— I enjoy doing Zumba and staying active.

— My wife, Carlin, and I traveled to Australia, New
Zealand, and visited our son who is married and living in the Czech Republic.

— I'm active in local and international politics, working
to make a better world for our children, grandchildren, and all future generations.

I remember the movie *Network,* and the fictional T.V. anchor-
man Howard Beale when he loses it on camera and shouts, "I'm
mad as hell, and I'm not going to take this anymore!" Many of us
remember him as a guy who went off the rails and "lost it." But
we forget what he was so crazy mad about. There were good reasons he was "mad as hell" and they are the same reasons many
of us today are fed up and angry at the state of our world. Here
are some of the common things I'm feeling and also hearing from
friends and clients:

— Our economic system isn't working well for people.
Most of us are working hard and harder, but we feel
we're not getting ahead. It seems the system favors
those with wealth and power, and the rest of us are
at a serious disadvantage.

— Our political system is often gridlocked, and the
average American does not feel well represented by
those in government.

— Our environment is suffering. Extreme weather causes drought in one place and flooding in others. The demands of industrial civilization are at odds with the environment, and our life-support system is in danger of collapse.

— There is a lack of civility among neighbors, communities, and countries. We seem at odds with each other, and problems become increasingly more difficult to solve.

— We face greater health challenges and our healthcare system does not seem able to truly provide the kind of care and support we need throughout our lives.

Getting "mad as hell" can be a positive reaction to conditions that are intolerable. Anger can energize us to reach out to each other for support and to work together to bring about positive change in our world. As we age, we learn to handle our anger more effectively. We can use it for the common good, rather than in endless cycles of blaming and shaming.

Why Is This Important? We can become preoccupied with our own personal miseries, our own aches and pains, or we can recognize the Power of Two, get connected, and work with others to change the world for the better. What needs changing in your neck of the woods? You don't have to do everything. You just need to do something that speaks to you. We all have life experiences that prepare us to make a difference at this time of life. Jump on board. It will feel good. Hope is a radical act, a commitment to a better future we all want.

Step 7: Learn what to do when both partners are going through the change of life.

Menopause in women and manopause in men happen around the same time of life, so it's not uncommon for men and women to be going through the changes together. Of course, similar issues are present when gay or lesbian couples go through the change of life. I was prepared, somewhat, for my wife's menopause. I tried to be understanding and compassionate, but I had a difficult time with her mood fluctuations, getting angry one minute and withdrawn the next. I also was unhappy about the negative impact it had on our sex life. Sometimes she wasn't interested, other times she was interested, but intercourse hurt, no matter what lubrication we tried.

Sometimes she seemed hypersexual and wanted me *now*. I had dreamed of her being so turned on. "I've got to have it now. Take me." But in reality it wasn't always comfortable for me. It seemed we were more often out of sync with each other, both sexually and emotionally. She wanted closeness when I wanted distance. When I hungered for more loving time together, she seemed to be off in her own world with friends and colleagues.

Carlin had similar problems with me going through menopause, but it took us both awhile before we accepted that my changes were as real as hers. Once we recognized what we were going through we could support each other with a greater sense of humor. In wasn't easy, but it helped to know that we both could be triggered by waves of emotions that would seemingly hit us out of the blue.

One of my colleagues, Nancy Cetel, MD, wrote a book, *Double Menopause: What to Do When Both You and Your Mate Go Through Hormonal Changes Together*. It helped Carlin and I recognize that we were both in this together. It enabled us to be more understanding of our own changes as well as our partner's. Lisa Friedman Bloch and Kathy Kirkland Silverman wrote *Manopause: Your Guide to Surviving His Change of Life*, which offers an important perspective on how the male "change of life" impacts a guy and his partner. This is truly a time where the Power of Two can bring us together or tear us apart.

This is a time that can bring out the best in us. It can also bring out the worst. Being compassionate, caring, and keeping a sense of humor can go a long way to helping us survive and thrive in this major life transition.

Nine

Life Stresses: Families, Money, a Collapsing Economy, and Our Collective Future

When Carlin and I met more than thirty-six years ago, it seemed like a simple story. She was traveling from her home in Oregon for a vacation in Mexico. She stopped to see friends in California, who invited her to the dojo where they practiced Aikido. Because she had done some Aikido in Oregon, she enjoyed the practice. Her friend thought we might like each other and introduced her to me. But like all stories, ours had its share of twists and turns.

I had recently gotten out of a very dysfunctional and dangerous marriage, and I was wary of women. (My ex-wife slept with a gun under her pillow to protect her from "men." That was not reassuring to me.) Carlin seemed like a nice woman, but my shields were on maximum protection mode and I did little more than smile politely and say, "Nice to meet you," before shifting my focus back to the martial arts practice.

Two weeks later I arrived in San Diego to attend a week-long community workshop with psychologist Jack Gibb on Trust Theory. I wanted to learn to trust more fully, but I had been burned twice before in two previous marriages and I knew I wasn't ready to try getting close to another woman. The TORI (stands for Trust, Openness, Realization, and Interdependence) offered an experience with a group that seemed a lot safer than what might happen between two people.

I was a bit shocked and surprised to see Carlin show up at the registration desk where I was volunteering. "Remember me?" she asked. "I'm Susan's friend. We met at the dojo in Mill Valley."

"Sure," I said, "Welcome to TORI." She got settled in and I went back to work. But something stirred in me, an attraction and a fear. I told myself in no uncertain terms, "Do not even consider getting involved with anyone. Sure she's nice, but nice can turn to hot and hot can burn your house down . . . with you in it."

There were hundreds of people at the workshop so Carlin's and my path didn't cross much. (Carlin says our paths crossed a lot, but I didn't notice.) But when they did, I felt a draw, which I resisted tenaciously until Carlin finally stopped me from running. "Listen, I've been dropping my hanky again and again and you don't seem to even notice. What's going on?" We talked and the talking went on for hours. She got that I had been hurt deeply, but so had she. We told each other about our two previous marriages and about our children. We had a lot in common.

As so often happens when we fall in love, there comes a moment where the rest of the world recedes into the background and there's just *The Two of Us*. Everything seems simple. Two people are in love. What else matters? Of course, if you get past the "in love" stage, there's a lot that matters including children, ex-spouses, money, grandchildren, and more. Here are some things we learned along the way. But we were in love and the rest of our lives seemed to fade into the background.

We spent the rest of the week at the TORI getting to know each other. It was the first time in my life that a woman had pursued me. I had always been the pursuer. Now it excited me to be wanted and sought after, and it also frightened me. I felt pulled out of my comfort zone, which Carlin has now been doing to me for more than thirty-six years.

The fact that she lived in Portland, Oregon, and I lived in Larkspur, California, made our courtship both safer and more exciting. We had long conversations on the phone, and I visited her and she visited me. Our love developed and deepened over a period of months. Soon we decided to merge our lives and Carlin moved to California. Then the real excitement began.

Step 1: Recognize that merging two lives is more complicated than we expect.

During the "falling-in-love" stage things seemed simple, but once we bonded and began building a life together, things got a lot more complicated. I had been living with Ken, one of the guys in my men's group. When I told him I had fallen in love with Carlin and she wanted to move to California, he graciously invited her to move into his house with us. When I told him she had a five-year-old son named Aaron, he never missed a beat welcoming the little guy into his home and we became a somewhat unusual family constellation.

I had just started a new job as the clinical director of a local drug and alcohol treatment program and became immersed in my work. Carlin got busy getting Aaron enrolled in school and we began our California life together. It wasn't easy on anyone. I went from being a single guy living with my buddy to being in a relationship with a young mother and her child. Carlin uprooted herself and her son and merged her life with mine and Ken's. Aaron seemed to be settling in well, and Ken opened his heart and home to an expanded family.

As Carlin and I had each been married twice before, we had fairly complicated lives, but all of us have complicated lives of one kind or another. As more and more of us divorce and remarry these complications must be understood, addressed, and grown with. We can never anticipate the full extent of the life we are choosing when we fall in love and commit to living with and loving another. But our higher power, deeper spirit, God, Goddess, or whatever we call that power has more in store for us than we could ever imagine.

Why Is This Important? When we fall in love and bond with another person, we soon feel the power and passion of two. However, each of the partners in the relationship has a rich history of connections that soon become a part of the pair. The matrix of connections expands greatly. If we're not prepared for the expansion we can feel overwhelmed. With inevitable "family crises," the relationship is continually tested. Each crisis is a lesson to be learned—an opportunity to learn more about ourselves, each other, and our journey together through life.

Step 2: Deal with children—yours, mine, and ours.

When Carlin and I first got together we talked about our children. She had three sons from her two previous marriages. I had a son and a daughter from my first marriage. When Carlin moved in with Aaron I had a chance to connect with a very bright and engaging five-year-old. But connecting with him also brought up conflicts in me. How would my two children feel about me having another child in our lives, as well as a new woman? If I got close to Aaron would my other children feel pushed out? If I bonded with Aaron would I be taking something away from the bond Carlin and Aaron had with each other? Did I want to be a stepfather to a child, and what did that mean? I knew how precious the relationship between father and son was. I didn't want to interfere with the connection Aaron had with his biological father.

Things got even more complicated when my daughter, Angela, came to live with us a year and a half later. She was ten years old at the time. She had been having a rough time with her mother, my ex. My first wife and I had adopted Angela when she was two and a half months old and Angela and her brother, Jemal, had been living with my ex following our divorce. Things had gotten increasingly difficult at home and it seemed necessary for Angela to come live with Carlin and me.

Angela felt displaced and angry. She was sure that Carlin would reject her and she did everything she could to push Carlin away to "prove" that she was not wanted. Carlin refused to give in to Angela's fears, even though Angela pushed her to her limits and beyond. "I care about you and I'm just not going to reject you, no matter what you do," Carlin told her. And she demonstrated it by her actions.

Over the years together Angela came to love Carlin deeply, and their bond remains strong to this day. Aaron and I also developed a deep connection. Among the many memories he and I share was being thrown together in a blanket as part of a young man's rite of passage weekend given by the Mankind Project, which Aaron and I attended when he was eighteen years old.

Although Carlin's two older sons, Dane and Evan, and my son, Jemal, never lived with us, we have all connected over the years. What began as *her* kids and *my* kids have evolved to *our* kids over the years. We now have fifteen grandchildren. For the most part we've managed to integrate our lives and our families. But it can be a real challenge.

It's said that no matter how long you were married, if you divorce you have an "ex" forever. We found that children continue to have needs and have challenges in their own lives. Often we've had to deal with our former spouses, sometimes directly, sometimes through the kids who may be having conflicts with their parent. Children growing up and becoming adults don't make those problems go away.

All in all, we found that family ties are dynamic and changing, but they make demands on our lives. We have had to learn to set good boundaries and protect the integrity of Carlin and I. Sometimes we've had to say "no" to children or grandchildren, or take time to ourselves when they wanted to see us. Other times Carlin and I would have to dive in to our old families to deal with issues that needed our involvement. It's never easy, but it's one of the cornerstones to developing and maintaining a deeper relationship between Carlin and me.

Why Is This Important? Children can pull a relationship apart or they can add roots of love, compassion, and magic. The children have tested us and, I'm sure, we have tested them. We've all grown more loving as a result of our lives together and apart. But, over time, families increase in size. This adds complexity that can sink a marriage. It's required a great deal of heart, soul, tears, and patience to deal with it all. If marriage is the graduate school of life, having children is surely the postgraduate training. And grandchildren are the diploma that some of us receive for getting through the program alive, but these kinds of diplomas don't hang passively on a wall. They have needs, and challenges, of their own. It's a great gift to be there for your family, and it requires great wisdom to say, "I can't do it. I'm sorry. I'm tapped out."

Step 3: Understand the real meaning of money.

I guess there might be some people who don't have issues around money. But if there are, I've never met them. Most of our money issues begin early in our lives. I grew up in a family where money was always scarce. As far back as I can remember my mother worked to support the family, even when my father was at home. But after he left, she had to work even harder to put food on the table and keep a roof over our head. I began doing odd jobs to make money when I was eight or nine years old.

I still remember my mother talking with her female friends about the out-of-work men when I was four years old. I can't remember exactly what they said, but I can still remember the pity, resentment, and disappointment in their voices. My father was out of work, and I felt a deep shame. I learned early that a man's main job was to support his family. A woman might choose to work, but if she *had* to work because the man couldn't, it meant he wasn't really a man.

I made a vow as a four-year-old boy that I would never let women talk to me like they were talking about my father and the unemployed men in the neighborhood. I told myself I would die first. Money for me, and most of us, was more than having the things that money could buy. It was about identity and manhood. If we had money, we could support our families. If we could do that, our lives meant something. If we couldn't, we were total and absolute failures and didn't deserve to be alive.

In our money-oriented culture, men are trained from an early age to be the bread-winners. Women are trained to believe that it's a man's job to provide. It's her job to spend the money he makes wisely. Even when women share the work world with men, these old beliefs still have a powerful influence on our lives. Being consumers is the mark of family that is supporting the society. In the aftermath of 9/11, President Bush encouraged all Americans to go shopping as usual and not to let terrorists alter our way of life.

But the era of mass consumerism is coming to an end. We can no longer live on a finite planet with finite resources and base our lives on consumption. Our economy is in transition and our old ways of looking at money are changing. As a result, there are also more conflicts around money. The era where one wage-earner could make enough to support a middle-class lifestyle is long past. Now both members of the marriage must work. But usually one person brings in more than the other.

Usually the man makes more money, but that is changing as women's salaries are increasing. Some men are choosing to spend time at home with children while the woman works. Whoever is earning the money, there can be conflicts. I've worked with men who resent the fact that their wives don't earn enough. I also have clients who, like my mother and her friends, resent the fact that the man isn't earning enough.

But income is only half of the equation. We still have to decide how we will spend our money. Again, there are often conflicts over how the money is spent. Some people are paying spousal or child support from previous marriages, which adds to the complexity of the issues. Plus, we all have different experiences and philosophies about money. Some people believe that we should spend it if we have it. Others feel it is important to save for a rainy day.

Finally (all though there's never really a *finally* when we talk about money), no matter what we work out today, there will likely be changes in the future. Just when we think we've worked out a plan that we can live with, something changes and we have to re-evaluate everything.

Why Is This Important? Most marriage and family counselors recognize that couples often have conflicts over two issues: sex and money. We likely have other disagreements, but sex and money seem to be perennial favorites. I think the main reason there is so much conflict is that we invest so much of our identity in these issues. If we're not having the sex life we want, we not only feel deprived of the pleasure we're missing, but even more important, we feel some essential part of our identity is missing. The same is true for money. If we don't have enough or if we don't feel our partner is bringing in or giving enough, we feel our very being is undermined. So when we have concerns about money, we need to understand that the roots of our concern go deep. We need to have compassion for ourselves, our partners, and the partnership itself.

Step 4: Accept that employment and unemployment will have new meanings for us.

I often counsel men and women who have lost their jobs. Usually, it hits the men harder than the women. Though women may feel the loss of income, they don't usually feel the job loss as a statement about their womanhood. For many men, if they lose their job it cuts to the core of their very identity.

This reality came home to me a few years ago when I lost my job as a counselor in a local health clinic. I had been on staff for more than eight years and economic changes forced the administration to cut back. When my contract was terminated, my conscious mind understood the realities, but my heart and soul were deeply wounded. I knew I would find another job, but I went into a deep depression. I couldn't shake the feeling that I'd failed and I felt a sense of shame I knew wasn't rational, but nevertheless it laid me low.

In her book *Stiffed: The Betrayal of the American Man*, Susan Faludi interviewed many men who had lost their jobs due to economic cut-backs. Like me, they often felt unemployment as a deep wound to their identity as a man. One of the men Faludi quoted in her book, Don Motta, could be speaking for millions of men in this country who have been laid off, downsized, or part of a company that has gone under. "There is no way you feel like a man. You can't," says Motta. "It's the fact that I'm not capable of supporting my family. . . . When you've been very successful in buying a house, a car, and could pay for your daughter to go to college, though she didn't want to, you have a sense of success and people see it. I haven't been able to support my daughter. I haven't been able to support my wife."[1] "I'll be very frank with you," he said slowly, placing every word down as if it were an increasingly heavy weight. "I . . . feel . . . I've . . . been . . . castrated."[2] Motta is clear about the connection among manhood, work, and sexuality. A man who can't work and support his family is a man without balls—not really a man at all.

The economic changes impacting us are likely to continue. Boadie W. Dunlop, MD, writing in the prestigious *British Journal of Psychiatry*, says, "The recent recession afflicting Western economies serves as a harbinger of the economic future for men."[3] In an economy in which unemployment will become an increasing reality for more and more men, we need to recognize that losing our job is not a personal failing, but a societal problem. Yet, it will take a great deal of support and understanding to help men realize that their identity is not wrapped up in their work, and losing their jobs says nothing about their value as a man.

Why Is This Important? In 2011 I was interviewed for a *Newsweek* cover story, "Dead Suit Walking: Can Manhood Survive the Recession?" The article recognized that even educated men with well-paying jobs were cast aside as the economy was collapsing.[4] Although the economy is recovering, it seems likely that we will face increasing unemployment in the future and we need to start right away to expand our base of worthiness to include other things than our jobs. We need to feel valued as a loving father, husband, friend, and neighbor—regardless of our job status.

Step 5: Learn to live with the collapse of an unsustainable economic system.

When men are out of work, we tend to take it personally. We question our own adequacy and identity. But the economic changes we are seeing are part of a larger change going on in the world. Václav Havel, former president of the Czech Republic, recognized the coming changes in a talk he gave at Independence Hall, in Philadelphia, on July 4, 1994. "Today, many things indicate that we are going through a transitional period, when it seems that something is on the way out and something else is painfully being born. It is as if something were crumbling, decaying and exhausting itself, while something else, still indistinct, were arising from the rubble."[5]

I got my first glimpse of the momentous changes that were impacting our lives in a Sweat Lodge Ceremony with twenty other men at the Wingspan Men's Conference in 1995. During the Sweat Lodge I had a vision where I saw the sinking of the Ship of Civilization and the survival of millions of linked lifeboats. Today we see these changes reflected in continuing economic disruptions all over the world and the emergence of Transition Town and Economic Localization movements. Here are some of the important things I've learned since my experiences in 1995:

We need to open our hearts and minds to the reality of massive change.

"People don't seem to realize it that it is not like we're on the *Titanic* and we have to avoid the iceberg," says Rob Watson, CEO and chief scientist of The EcoTech International Group, who Pulitzer Prize–winning author Tom Friedman calls one of the best environmental minds in America. "We've already hit the iceberg. The water is rushing in down below. But some people just don't want to leave the dance floor; others don't want to give up on the buffet. But if we don't make the hard choices, nature will make them for us."[6] We need to understand that there is a good life for us beyond civilization.

When I first had the vision of the sinking Ship of Civilization it scared the hell out of me. Are we going to go back to using a spear to hunt for food and gathering roots and grubs? I've learned that things are changing, but letting go of an unsustainable system that has been exploiting the earth and most of the people is not a bad thing.

Writing in 1987, Pulitzer Prize–winning author Jared Diamond says the agricultural revolution that began 10,000 years ago may have been "the worst mistake in the history of the human race."[7] Visionary author Daniel Quinn says, "Because it's intrinsically hierarchical, civilization benefits members at the top very richly but benefits the masses at the bottom very poorly—and this has been so from the beginning."[8] But civilization is not the end of the road as many fear, but just the beginning, as Quinn reminds us in his book *Beyond Civilization: Humanity's Next Great Adventure.*

In the face of big changes, learn not to panic.

We are experiencing massive changes in the world, but humans have been through big change before and we need not panic. In order to be around for the next chapter we are going to have to adapt and become comfortable with the unknown. The serenity prayer,[9] originally written by philosopher Reinhold Niebuhr and adopted by Alcoholics Anonymous, can be a powerful reminder.

God grant me the serenity
To accept the things I cannot change;
Courage to change the things I can;
And wisdom to know the difference.

Put your roots down in a community.

With big changes coming, we need the support of a local community. Things may get dicey at the international, national, and state levels. So, putting down roots in a local community is vital. One of the reasons Carlin and I moved to Willits was to join with others to enjoy the adventure that Daniel Quinn describes in *Beyond Civilization.* Willits was one of the first towns in the country to develop a structure and plan so that we will survive and thrive. You can learn more about what we're doing here in Willits by visiting our website: *www.well95490.org/*.

Join a tribe for mutual support.

We often think of tribal culture as being dead and gone, but tribes are as essential today as they were in times past. "The people of our culture don't want to acknowledge that the tribe is for humans exactly what the pod is for whales or the troop is for baboons: the gift of millions of years of natural selection, not perfect—but damned hard to improve upon," says Daniel Quinn. In his book *Tribes,* business guru Seth Godin says a tribe is a group of people connected to each other, to a leader and to an idea.[10] Find your tribe and put down roots in your local community.

Carlin and I helped create "the Village circle," a group of twelve men and women who have been meeting together for ten years and offer and receive mutual support. Once a month we get together to share rituals of connection and healing, create a meal together, and enjoy each other's company.

David Korten, author of *The Great Turning: From Empire to Earth Community,* calls us to step up our commitment to changing our present economic system. "To create a world in which life can flourish and prosper," says Korten, "we must replace the values and institutions of capitalism with values and institutions that honor life, serve life's needs, and restore money to its proper role as servant. I believe we are in fact being called to take a step to a new level of species consciousness and function."[11] In *WorldShift 2012: Making Green Business, New Politics, and Higher Consciousness Work Together,* Club of Budapest founder Ervin Laslo says, "We are involved in a shift from a path of unsustainability, conflict, and confrontation to a path toward sustainability, well-being, and peace."[12] This is a wonderful time to be alive.

Step 6: Understand that the new human vocation is to heal the earth.

Before we moved to Willits I was a city kid. I was born in New York City, was raised in Los Angeles, and spent much of my adult life in and around the San Francisco Bay area. I knew very little about the earth. When we moved to Willits and bought our home on twenty-two acres in the hills, everything scared me, including the bugs, the bees, and the bears, not to mention the inverter at the heart of our solar system, the chain saw, and the backup generator.

In the twenty-four years we've lived here, I've learned that I'm not a being separate from nature. I am a part of nature, as much a part as the bugs, the bees, and the bears. I've learned to enjoy sleeping out under the stars, walking barefoot on the ground, and learning to grow food from the earth.

Just as many of us have lost our creative connection to ourselves and each other, we've also lost our connection to the earth. When we think of that connection, we tend to think of "mother earth." But just as we've expanded our understanding of the deity by expanding our vision of "God the Father" to include the feminine, we can expand our vision of the earth to include the masculine. I've found that reconnecting to the earth can help us get back in touch with ourselves and remind us that the earth is the source of all life. By taking care of the earth, we take care of ourselves and all those we love.

Thomas Berry was a priest, a "geologian," and a historian of religions. He spoke eloquently to our connection to the earth and the consequences of our failure to remember we are one member in the community of life: "We never knew enough. Nor were we sufficiently intimate with all our cousins in the great family of the earth. Nor could we listen to the various creatures of the earth, each telling its own story. The time has now come, however, when we will listen or we will die."[13] These words continue to reverberate through my being: **"The time has come when we will listen, or we will die."** It's hard to listen when we simply see the earth as our own private larder. Whatever we need or want, we feel we have a right to go in and take whatever tickles our fancy. We don't realize how crazy that is. It would be like the brain deciding it needs more nutrients because "I am in charge" and taking more and more from the heart, liver, and kidneys. It's clear to me that we need a change of perception, and we need it right away.

I've taken strength and wisdom from the words of social psychologist and writer Sam Keen. His words offer simple guidance to the work we have to do: "The radical vision of the future rests on the belief that the logic that determines either our survival or our destruction is simple:

1. The new human vocation is to heal the Earth.
2. We can only heal what we love.
3. We can only love what we know.
4. We can only know what we touch."[14]

As I'm learning more about the earth, I'm also learning to heal myself, love myself, know myself, and get more deeply in touch with my feelings to guide my steps during these turbulent times.

Why Is This Important? The world is becoming increasingly complex, and it's difficult to get our heads around all the things that grab our attention in the news each day. It's easy to become overwhelmed. I've found keeping things simple and focused on what I can do to heal the part of the world that is given to me allows me to make a difference. If each of us focused on what we could do to heal our own part of the world, together we could bring humans back in alignment with the rest of nature.

Ten

In Sickness and in Health: Caregiving and Receiving

I grew up worrying about my health and the health of those I love. It could be that my worry began even before I was born. Let me explain. My mother and father got married on her birthday, October 5, 1934, in Greenwich Village. They both wanted children but were unsuccessful. They'd nearly given up hope when they learned of an experimental technique of injecting the father's sperm into the mother's womb. I was conceived in mid-March 1943.

My mother told stories about walking gingerly down the streets of New York, afraid she'd dislodge the developing fetus. She said she worried that she would lose me before I was born. However, I made it into the world December 21, 1943. My parent's worries weren't over, not by a long shot. I was a small child, and my mother was always afraid that something would happen to me. I developed respiratory problems early on, perhaps from the second-hand smoke I inhaled from their cigarettes. Some of my earliest memories were of my mother collecting Raleigh cigarette coupons along with her S&H Green Stamps.

She was so concerned about "something happening to my baby" that she wouldn't let my father hold me. She said she was afraid he'd drop me. And her worries didn't end with me. She was thirty-four years old when I was born, and she was constantly worried that she would die before I reached a certain age. I remember her worries that she wouldn't make it until I graduated high school. Then she wasn't sure I'd make it through college before she kicked off. She actually lived to the age of eighty.

Throughout my life I became preoccupied with staying healthy. My wife, Carlin, had a similar focus based on her early experiences. Her mother related to her children much better when they were sick than when they were healthy. She wanted to take Carlin and her brothers to the doctor all the time for this suspected ailment or that. This is now known as Munchausen by proxy syndrome (MBPS) and is seen as a way for a parent to get attention and support from medical personnel. In Carlin's home, you only got love and attention if you were sick.

Early on Carlin made a decision that she would not give in to her mother's needs. She chose to be well and had to forego the maternal attention that her mother gave to Carlin's brothers. Where as I liked the added attention I received from my mother when I was sick, for Carlin it was the only way to get attention. Both Carlin and I have focused a lot on staying healthy throughout our lives. One of the great gifts I have received from Carlin, though at times I resisted it, was that I got rewarded for being well, and got much less attention when I was sick.

Understanding health and illness is important throughout our lives. As we get older, it takes on new meanings and added importance. Getting older is much more fun when we're healthy. Of course, we need nurturing, care, and support when we do get sick, but we don't want to focus so much on illness that our lives revolve around our ills. Finding the right balance between care when we're sick and support when we're healthy is not always easy. Here are some of the things we've learned over the years.

Step 1: Let go of the myth that getting sick is an inevitable part of aging.

As I've gotten older I hear a lot of my friends and clients talking about the inevitable health problems that we face as we age. I don't believe it. My mother was preoccupied with illness her whole life. I've tried not to follow in her footsteps.

I'll be seventy-two this year and I feel wonderful. My attitude is that health is the default setting of my body/mind/spirit (I call this unified totality The BMS). The BMS is a wonderfully designed system that is constantly working to keep us in balance with life. If we follow the "owner's manual" guidelines it will serve us well and allow us to live out our full life span in total health.

Too many of us have learned negative attitudes about health and aging. Some people see illness and disease as an inevitable part of life. They just assume that some people naturally get sick. "I inherited my mother's sensitive stomach," one woman told me. "I always get sick after I eat." For years, I told myself that I inherited my father's mental illness. It has taken me a long time to realize that I have control over my body, mind, and spirit, and no illness is inevitable.

Other people have negative attitudes about getting old. They see themselves the victim of the added years. They fear turning forty, and turning fifty is even worse. They often associate aging with illness. But it doesn't have to be that way. What are your beliefs about aging and illness? Are you holding any old beliefs that may be interfering with your ability to live long and well?

Why Is This Important? We know that our beliefs are powerful. They can keep us healthy, and they can make us sick. Often negative, unexamined beliefs reside in our subconscious. We may not even be aware they are there. They are like computer programs operating in the background. They can have a profound influence on our lives, but we don't know they are taking us in the wrong directions. Bringing these subconscious beliefs into awareness is the first step to reversing them.

Step 2: Learn to think and act like people who live long and well.

There have been numerous studies of long-lived peoples. I think they are helpful to give us an idea of how long we're designed to live. They can also teach us what works to stay alive and well through the years. In 2004, Dan Buettner teamed up with *National Geographic* and the world's best longevity researchers to identify pockets around the world where people live measurably longer and better. In these "Blue Zones" (Loma Linda, California; Nocoya, Costa Rica; Sardinia, Italy; Ikaria, Greece; and Okinawa, Japan), they found that people reach age 100 at rates 10 times greater than in the general population of the United States. They found that the lifestyles of all Blue Zones residents shared nine specific characteristics. Buettner and his team also learned about things we can all do:

Movement is a natural part of life.

They live in places where they can walk to the store, to their friend's house, or places of worship. Their houses have stairs. They have gardens in their yards.

 What you can do: To start moving naturally, consider making things a little more difficult. Take that extra trip up or down the stairs instead making it all in one trip. Walk to your airport gate instead of taking the moving walkway or park far from the entrance when you visit a store. Walk a dog, do your own yard and housework, and walk around your town.

They have a life purpose that engages them.

Knowing your sense of purpose is worth up to seven years of extra life expectancy. The Okinawans call it *ikigai* and the Nicoyans call it *plan de vida*—for both, it translates to "why I wake up in the morning."

What you can do: Begin investigating your own purpose by reflecting on your own life. What excites you? What needs doing in the world that you feel called on to engage? Is there a purpose you and your life partner share that you could engage together?

They shed their stress.

Chronic stress leads to chronic inflammation, which is associated with every major age-related disease. Although everyone experiences stress, the world's longest-lived people have routines to shed that stress. Okinawans take a few moments each day to remember their ancestors, Adventists pray, Ikarians take a nap, and Sardinians do happy hour.

What you can do: Make stress relief a priority. I did and wrote a book about it, *Stress Relief for Men* (works for women, too). Like the long-lived and healthy *Blue Zoners*, you need to build regular practices into your life.

They keep their weight down.

According to the National Institutes of Health, more than two-thirds (68.8 percent) of adults are considered to be overweight or obese.[1] We tend to gauge ourselves by those around us. Doing that keeps us fat. If most of those we see around us are overweight, we have a tendency to follow suit. *Blue Zoners* don't have to try and lose weight. They are surrounded by family, friends, and neighbors who live a healthy lifestyle.

What you can do: We can all do our best to lose weight on our own, but it will work much better to make it a family project, a neighborhood project, or a project of your whole town.

They eat mostly plant-based foods.

Food expert Michael Pollan captures the essence of what these communities do when he was asked what should humans eat in order to be maximally healthy. His simple response: Eat food. Not too much. Mostly plants.

What you can do: We are surrounded by a corporate food culture that wants us to become addicted to the **Modern American Diet**. They want us to eat fast food, processed foods, and unhealthy foods because they are profitable. For an insightful and engaging look at how the food giants hooked us, I recommend you read Pulitzer Prize–winning author Michael Moss's book, *Salt, Sugar, Fat: How the Food Giants Hook Us,* and then commit to finding people who will join you in eating more fruits, vegetables, and beans.

They enjoy a glass or two of wine with dinner.

Thanks to healthy plant compounds and antioxidants, wine has been shown to reduce the risk of heart disease, and certain cancers, and slow the progression of neurological disorders like Alzheimer's and Parkinson's disease. Every culture enjoys a social lubricant of some kind. Wine is traditional and, when used in moderation, it can add to your enjoyment of life.

What you can do: Honor the words of our founding father Benjamin Franklin who said, "Wine is constant proof that God loves us and loves to see us happy."

They know the value of tribes.

Daniel Quinn, author of *Ishmael* and *Beyond Civilization*, reminds us that the tribe is the basic unit for human communities. "The tribal life doesn't turn people into saints," says Quinn. "It enables ordinary people to make a living together with a minimum of stress year after year, generation after generation."[2] The world's longest-lived people are either born into or choose to create social circles that support healthy behaviors. Ikarians enjoy tight-knit communities that socialize frequently. Okinawans build *moai* groups of five friends that commit to each other for life.

What you can do: Research from the Framingham Studies shows that smoking, obesity, happiness, and even loneliness are contagious.[3] If you don't already have one, put together a tribe committed to supporting each other's health. Assessing who you hang out with, and then proactively surrounding yourself with the right friends, will do more to add years to your life than just about anything else.

They all live in spirit-based communities.

All but five of the 263 centenarians interviewed in the original Blue Zones areas studies belonged to some faith-based community. It doesn't matter if you're Christian, Buddhist, Muslim, Jewish, or another religion. What matters is that you attend regularly and truly feel part of a larger group.

What you can do: Join a community that supports its members and has a connection to spirit and soul. If your traditional community doesn't uplift you, make you feel more loving, and connected to the larger world, find one that does.

They put their families first.

We live in a world that is more focused on material success and building wealth for the few than in supporting families. Start with the Power of Two and expand from there. Happy, healthy centenarians in the Blue Zones areas put their families first.

What you can do: This can take shape in many ways, from keeping your aging parents and grandparents in or near your home to being in a positive, committed relationship, which can add up to six years of life expectancy. Putting family first doesn't mean putting yourself last. You two are an important part of the family, and your needs count too.

The Blue Zones Project has additional suggestions that you and your community can engage in order to stay healthy. You can check them out here: *www.bluezonesproject.com /bluezones-communities#slide1*

Step 3: Engage the six practices that science says will prevent more than 80 percent of disease.

What would you do if I told you there was a way to slash your risk of heart disease, cancer, diabetes, and other diseases we fear by 80 percent or more? Would you be interested? I've been practicing healthy living for more than forty years, but my understanding and practice got a boost when I met David Katz, MD. Dr. Katz is an impressive guy, with a solid background. He's president of the American College of Lifestyle Medicine and the founding director of Yale University's Yale-Griffin Prevention Research Center. He's written a very helpful book, *Disease Proof: The Remarkable Truth About What Makes Us Well*. He has authored over 200 scientific papers and chapters, 15 books, and more than 1,000 columns and blogs.

He, and his colleagues, have found that there are six lifestyle factors that can reduce our risk of disease by more than 80 percent. He summarizes them as follows: feet, forks, fingers, sleep, stress, and social connections.

- Feet: Regular physical activity is associated with weight control, reduced inflammation, enhanced immune function, and reduced cancer risk specifically.
- Forks: An optimal diet exerts far-ranging effects on every aspect of physiology, and similarly stands to reduce the risk of all chronic disease.

— Fingers: Don't smoke, and if you do stop. Even though 80 percent of us have stopped, there is still 20 percent who haven't yet made the switch.

If you're engaging the three Fs, you are reducing your risk of disease by 80 percent. Add the three Ss and you can lower your risk even more.[4]

— Sleep: According to the Centers for Disease Control and Prevention (CDC), an estimated 50–70 million U.S. adults have sleep problems.[5] Sleep insufficiency is linked to motor vehicle crashes, industrial disasters, occupational errors, and medical problems. Persons experiencing sleep insufficiency are also more likely to suffer from chronic diseases such as hypertension, diabetes, depression, and obesity, as well as from cancer, increased mortality, and reduced quality of life and productivity. So, learn to get a good night's sleep and you will be healthier and happier throughout your life.

— Stress: We know that stress can kill us, and stress has more to do with our state of mind than the things that happen in our lives.

— Social connections: This whole book is about how we can develop real, lasting love with our partner. But we don't have to be married to gain the benefits of social connection. Deeping our friendships and our social bonds can offer health benefits as well. I've been in a men's group that has been meeting regularly for thirty-six years. These guys are like brothers, only better. We choose to be together and support each other through all the challenges of life. My wife, Carlin, is also in a women's group. I think same-sex groups are vital to our well-being. They are part of our hunter–gatherer legacy, and they are even more important today. Carlin and I are also part of the "village circle," a group of men and women who come together every month for celebration, ritual, and support.

Why Is This Important? There is now ample scientifically sound evidence that engaging these six practices can reduce our risk of illness more than 80 percent. But there are no guarantees in life. We may do all the right things and still get sick. "Hey, my friend ate well, exercised, didn't smoke, and he still got cancer and died," one friend told me. "So why do all this healthy stuff? I might as well enjoy myself." He's got a point. Too many of us see health practices as being boring and not much fun. I've found we don't have to be fanatical about these things. I've been known to eat my share of hot fudge sundaes and those killer cookies that they make at the Brickhouse. But mostly taking care of myself is a challenge that I enjoy.

We all have a choice. We can do engage these six practices or give up and avoid them. Either way we'll live until we die. But the reality is that if we go against these six, we will probably live many years with chronic illness, which may be worse than death. There are no guarantees. Dr. Katz offers this bit of wisdom that I like:

"**Lifestyle practices are the ship and sails, but there is still the wind and waves.** The former we can control to increase the probability of a safe crossing; the latter, we cannot—and thus even a well-captained ship may founder."[6]

We must all learn to focus on the things we can change and to accept the mysteries of life that impact our health.

Step 4: Understand the root causes of heart problems, depression, and other health challenges.

By the time we get to midlife most of us have had to deal with both acute and chronic health problems. The dislocated shoulder

I got in high school causes me pain later in life, which I finally learned to heal with energy medicine techniques. Carlin and I have both had to deal with problems that are more complex and have deeper roots.

I've had to deal with depression and bipolar disorder throughout my life, and I have struggled with emotional ups and downs, irritability and anger, and breathing problems. A few years ago I started having heart arrhythmias, where my heart would speed up and miss beats. I've also had prostatitis and prostate enlargement.

I believe that illnesses and disease always contain information that can help me heal. I always look for the lessons my illnesses are trying to teach me. One of the most powerful lessons has been to recognize that many of our adult ailments are connected to the wounds from our childhood, which I described in Chapter 3.

It was difficult for me to believe, at first, that my father's suicide attempt when I was five or my parent's divorce could be responsible for physical and emotional illnesses that occurred years later. But that's what the original Adverse Childhood Experiences (ACE) Study demonstrated and thousands of studies since have validated. An eye-opening new book by award-winning scientific journalist Donna Jackson Nakazawa, *Childhood Disrupted: How Your Biography Becomes Your Biology, and How You Can Heal*, demonstrates the power of our childhood wounds to change our brains and even the way our genes are turned on or off.

We've all heard the old adage "What doesn't kill you makes you stronger." However, the research findings demonstrate that childhood trauma leads to lifelong struggles with mental and physical health. Take a look at your ACE score from Chapter 3. How many did you check? My ACE score was 4. For each ACE you checked your risk of developing later illness is increased. For instance, people with an ACE score of 4 are:

— Twice as likely to be smokers,
— Seven times more likely to be alcoholic,
— Four times more likely to develop emphysema or chronic bronchitis, and
— Twelve times more likely to attempt suicide.

People with high ACE scores are more likely to be violent, and to have more marriages, more broken bones, more drug prescriptions, more depression, and more autoimmune diseases. People with an ACE score of 6 or higher are at risk of their life span being shortened by twenty years.

Why Is This Important? Being aware of ACEs helps me better understand myself. It has allowed me to be easier on myself, when all my efforts to "eat well, exercise, do all the right things" didn't allow me to avoid illness. It also helped me take seriously the risks I had for problems and allowed me to make more of a commitment to my health. Having an increased risk of illness due to childhood trauma doesn't guarantee we will develop problems. I never smoked and I don't have a drinking problem. But I have dealt with other addictive behaviors, have had multiple marriages, and suffered from depression. I believe what I've done to stay healthy have helped, even though I continue to deal with health issues. Finally, it reminds us all about the importance of childhood health so that we can better protect our children, grandchildren, and all children.

Step 5: Embrace the good news that many health problems can be reversed using mind/body practices.

When I first learned about Blue Zones studies and things we can do to prevent health problems, I wished I had learned about these things sooner. Once we have problems, particularly ones that have become chronic, we often feel that there's little we can do about them. We either feel they are part of our genetic heritage and there's nothing we can do, or they have been with us for so long that there's nothing we can do.

The good news is that a whole body of research findings tells us that the mind and body are connected. We can even think of it as a single entity: Mind/Body. Whatever is going on in our minds, such as depression, can be healed through mind/body practices. And whatever may be going on in our bodies, whether it's heart problems or even cancer, can be healed through mind/body practices.

The fact that we can now reverse chronic conditions like heart disease, diabetes, and cancer has been proven by a number of researchers including Dean Ornish, MD, a friend and colleague of Dr. David Katz, who, we met earlier in the chapter. Dr. Ornish is the founder and president of the nonprofit Preventive Medicine Research Institute and clinical professor of Medicine at the University of California, San Francisco.

Dr. Ornish's thirty-seven years of research have scientifically proven that the integrative lifestyle changes he recommends can:

— Improve chronic conditions such as heart disease, diabetes, and prostate cancer;
— Change gene expression, turning on health-promoting genes and turning off disease-promoting genes; and
— Lengthen telomeres, the ends of chromosomes, which begins to reverse aging on a cellular level.

Says Dr. Ornish, "We focus on four elements of life: What you eat, how you respond to stress, how much activity you have, and how much love and support you have."[7] So we see that the same practices that can prevent disease can heal our diseases, even after they have become severe. That's good news for us all. Whether our disease has come from our childhood experiences, from lifestyle choices we have made, or from the pressures of life—we can do a lot to heal ourselves at any stage of the process.

Step 6: Learn to accept the entire journey of life, including death.

The joy of staying as healthy as we can and reversing disease has its own rewards, but one of them is not avoiding death. Two stories about death give me great hope as Carlin and I age. The first involves Carlin's mother, who moved in with us during the last months of her time dealing with cancer.

She spent most of her time in a bed we set up in our living room. I had not known her very well during the years Carlin and I had been together, though we visited for short times at her home in Oregon. But when she moved in with us and was facing death I felt like we developed a much deeper connection. We would talk and I would listen. Sometimes I just held her hand as we gazed out the window. In the last week of her life, she didn't talk much and I often sat with her gazing into her eyes. I felt it was like looking into the eyes of God. There was a peacefulness and joy that I felt being with her. It made we feel much less afraid about my own death.

The other story involved my father, who died rather suddenly. In the last years of his life he had been living alone in a small apartment in San Francisco. Each day he went out for a walk and he continued his "job" as a street puppeteer, putting on shows wherever people gathered. He rarely got sick. But one day I got a call from a nurse who told me he had contracted pneumonia and was in the local hospital.

I had been planning a Rite of Passage ceremony for our son Aaron. I had done this for each of our children when they turned twenty-one. I would take them anywhere in the country they wanted to go. My daughter, Angela, wanted to go to Chicago and meet Oprah. Aaron wanted to go to New Orleans for the Jazz

Festival. When I found out my father was in the hospital I was reluctant to go, but he encouraged me. "It's your son's time," he told me. "I'll be fine. Enjoy the music and think of me." His doctors also assured me that his pneumonia wasn't serious and I need not worry about being gone for a week.

When we arrived in New Orleans, I called home to see how things were. I was shocked to hear that my father had died hours after we left. I was heart-broken. I felt guilty for leaving my father, and my son and I grieved the loss. However, being in New Orleans, with its tradition of celebrating life and death, seemed like the place for us to be.

When we returned, I learned more about my father's passing. The nurse on the unit who had become close with my father told me about his last hour alive. "It was very strange," she told me. "I had come into his room to see how he was. He took off his oxygen mask and we talked. He seemed in good spirits. After talking a while he asked me if I'd leave the room and come back in fifteen minutes. I thought it was kind of a strange request, but I complied. I thought he might need some time alone or he might need to use the bathroom. When I came back into his room, he had died. We did all we could to bring him back, but he seemed to have passed peacefully."

Why Is This Important? I think we all deal with death differently. Being with Carlin's mom helped me recognize that dying is just another stage of life and one to be honored rather than feared. My father's death helped me see that we really can choose how and when we die. With my father's background as an actor, director, and writer, I can almost see him arranging the scenes of the play. "Okay, we've all got to die sometime. I'll plan to go out on the day that Jed's youngest son has his Rite of Passage into manhood. Yeah, that would be good. Now, where should we have it? I've got it, we'll have them be in New Orleans, perfect setting for a story that will be told over and over through the ages." My father was a story-teller and I do believe he would have liked to know that I'm telling this story to you. He might not have consciously arranged to die in this way, but he would have loved the story.

Step 7: Appreciate the blessings of partnership from beginning to end.

One of the great benefits of being married through the years is that we have an opportunity to deal with illness, injury, and ultimately death, together. I think most of us are less afraid of death than of being alone or feeling that our lives had no meaning. Being with your partner through all stages of life, including death, can be a great blessing.

Taking care of another who is ill, afraid, or in pain is a great gift of love. And when we are in the last period of our lives, it brings us closer to God, the Great Spirit, or whatever we believe is the ultimate manifestation of the divine.

When one of us gets sick, we're both sick, not only because we empathize with each other, but we actually share the illness together. It's a great blessing to be able to know we will be together for the whole journey. I've been there for Carlin when she dealt with breast cancer. She's been with me through my life-threatening adrenal tumor. And I trust that we will be together to the end. That's something definitely worth sticking around to see.

Eleven

Your Enlightened Future: Single Now, but Looking for Real, Lasting Love

*M*y great grandfather Charles was married eight times. He was my mother's, mother's father. I thought it was rather strange and wonderful that he had been married so many times. He lived until he was in his nineties, and he married for the last time when he was eighty-eight. I remember visiting him when I was a young boy. "A man isn't meant to be alone," he told me. "We're meant to go through life together." In his case, he had outlived his last two wives and he practiced his belief that a man shouldn't be alone by marrying again.

Another person who is a great role model for me is my friend Edie. She lives in my town of Willits and she's 107 years young. I mean that literally. She still walks around town, although she moves a bit slower in recent years. She has outlived a number of husbands, but not her desire to keep dancing. After her last husband died when he was in his eighties and she was well past one hundred, she put an ad in the local newspaper looking for another dance partner.

At the funeral of her last husband, I was talking to his brother. I asked about how he thought Edie would be. He told me, "Don't worry about Edie. She'll probably find another man again." Edie is that kind of person, full of life and a desire to connect with others.

The "singles scene" is changing a lot. As late-life marriage researcher Nancy Kalish, PhD, points out, "Men and women are living longer, and it is more normative to remarry after being widowed. In addition, divorces are common now for people of all ages, and these men and women often take new partners later in life. A bride and groom in the twenty-first century, or a senior gay couple who can now legally marry, are just as likely to be seventy-five as twenty-five; love and marriage are sought by people all ages.[1] We never know when we might lose our partner, through death or divorce. It can happen early on or late. Whenever it happens we all have to go through the grieving process, but then we begin to turn our attention to finding real, lasting love once again. It's never easy to grieve our losses or to move on to finding love again, but I believe it will always be worth doing. Here are the steps that I've found can guide you along the way.

Step 1: Review your past relationship history.

When a relationship ends, whether by divorce or death, we all go through the five stages of loss and grief first described by Elisabeth Kübler-Ross in her 1969 book *On Death and Dying*:

- Denial and isolation—We don't want to believe our relationship has ended and we close ourselves down and cut ourselves off from others.
- Bargaining—We have endless dialogues inside about "what if . . ." and try to figure out what went wrong and if somehow we could get the relationship back.
- Anger—We get waves of anger at the other person and at ourselves.

- Depression—We experience deep sadness and regret. We turn away from the world and live with our wounds.
- Acceptance—We come to peace with the loss and return to life anew.

We all go through the process differently. Some go step by step. Others jump around. Most of us go through the stages multiple times, and we each have our own time table for reaching acceptance. Some people get stuck in earlier stages and keep going around and around in anger or depression.

This is a good time to review our relationship history. Go back to your parents and think about their relationship with each other and what models, positive or negative, they offered. Look at your own relationship with key figures in your early life with family members. Ask how all these relationships may have affected your love map. Some people can do this on their own. Others find it helps to work with a therapist or guide.

Step 2: List the beliefs you have about yourself and marriage that can help you love again.

For a long while after my first divorce I was disoriented. I did well to get up in the morning, dress, and get on with my day. It took a number of years before I could begin understanding where my life was now, where I wanted it to be, and if I wanted to attempt to share it with another.

Looking back over those years I realize there were certain beliefs that were positive in helping me find real, lasting love. These included the following:

- I usually have an optimistic view toward life. I believe that the future can be better than the past.

- Even though my ex doesn't think highly of me, I'm a pretty good person.
- There are a lot of people in the world. Surely there must be someone I can love and who would love me.
- I'm more mature now than when I first married. I'll do better this time.
- Divorce is not the end of the world. Lots of people move on to a better life.

Make your own list. We all have some beliefs that are likely to help us find a partner and develop a loving relationship. What are yours?

Step 3: List the beliefs you have about yourself and marriage that can hinder you finding love again.

Even though I consider myself an optimist, I realized there were many beliefs I carried that interfered with my desire to find real, lasting love. Many of these beliefs were subconscious and they only surfaced gradually as I let myself be open to their influence. These beliefs included the following:

- Even if I find someone, they'll probably abandon me.
- In the long run, relationships just don't last.
- You can't really trust women.
- I don't trust my judgment. I'll probably make the same mistakes again.
- There is really only one right person for each of us. I blew my one chance and I'll have to live with it.
- My parents got divorced and never found someone better. Why try?
- I don't want to hurt my children. I'd better put my attention on them and forget about another relationship.

Again, make your own list. Dig deep and see how many of your own limiting beliefs you can uncover. Just knowing they are there gives you an opportunity to change them.

Step 4: Feed the "good wolf" that supports real, lasting love.

My wife, Carlin, is part Native American with roots in the Cherokee tradition. There is a story about two wolves that illustrates the way competing belief systems can occupy our minds.

One evening an old Cherokee told his grandson about a battle that goes on inside people. He said, "My son, the battle is between two wolves inside us all. One is Evil—it is anger, envy, fear, jealousy, sorrow, regret, greed, arrogance, self-pity, guilt, resentment, inferiority, lies, false pride, superiority, and ego. The other is Good—it is joy, peace, love, hope, serenity, humility, kindness, benevolence, empathy, generosity, truth, compassion and faith."

The grandson thought about what his grandfather had said. Finally he asked, "Which wolf wins?"

The wise grandfather simply replied, "The one that you feed."

Carlin and I often do a meditation where we imagine we are on a bridge with a stream running beneath. We imagine we let go of all the things that interfere with our joy, our anger, envy, fear, and so on. We picture ourselves throwing into the stream (or putting them into a nice boat) and letting the stream gently carry them away. You might imagine that you could put all your negative beliefs that block you from finding real, lasting love, "the bad" wolf, into that boat.

Now imagine you embrace all the positive beliefs that support you finding real, lasting love and bring each of them into your heart. In this way you feed "the good wolf."

Why Is This Important? If we've been through the ending of a relationship, we all carry beliefs that served to protect us from being hurt again. For me, beliefs like "In the long run, relationships just don't last," kept me from jumping into another relationship too soon and making the same mistakes again. But holding on to these negative beliefs keeps us from taking the risk to reach out again. We forget there are also risks in depriving ourselves of a partner with whom we can share real, lasting love. Both Carlin and I had to "throw the old negative beliefs over the bridge" before we could be ready to find each other. I see too many people enter a new relationship, but deep down inside they are sure it won't work out. Don't do that to yourself. Carlin and I found real, lasting love, on the third go-round. You can too, no matter how many relationships have ended for you in the past.

Step 5: Heal the wounds of betrayal.

No matter how our relationship ended, whether through separation, divorce, or death, there are feelings of betrayal. Our partner may have lied, cheated, or stolen. Or they may be been a paragon of virtue who simply died. We may have been the one who ended the relationship. It doesn't matter how it happened. We will have to deal with the wounds of betrayal.

The bonds of love begin for all of us even before we are born. Our desire for a loving and secure connection with those we depend upon for life is built into each of us. When that bond is threatened, we suffer.

Even in utero, my mother was afraid I wasn't firmly attached and she walked around New York worrying that she would lose the baby. I came into the world with a felt perception of insecurity. My mother's fear that she wouldn't live until I grew up added to my fears.

When I got married, I thought I had finally found someone I could count on, who wouldn't die, and who wouldn't leave me. When that dream ended I felt like my world came crashing down. Not only did I feel betrayed and abandoned by my wife, but that I'd been betrayed and abandoned by life.

Healing was a gradual process, facilitated by a number of good therapists, who allowed me to work through my feelings and to get comfortable again in my body. Other processes that I've found helpful include the following:

- Writing—You don't have to be a professional writer to let your feelings of betrayal flow. Getting it out and on paper can be tremendously healing.
- Drawing—Make a collage, or express your feelings through art.
- Practice mindfulness meditation—Just being present with yourself can heal old wounds.
- Get moving—Walking, Tai Chi, Qigong, and Aikido can all help you reconnect with your body.
- Practice loving kindness—Finding ways to express your love with people you feel safe with can be healing. Helping older people or children can be healing for you.

Why Is This Important? It's impossible to allow our positive beliefs to guide our lives as long as we continue to be caught in the undercurrent of unhealed betrayal. The feelings are so painful that most of us want to avoid them at all cost, but going in and healing them can be the key that gets us on the path to a world of real, lasting love. Remember, Carlin and I each had two failed marriages before we got back on the path and found each other. We've now been together for thirty-six wonderful years and are looking forward to continuing to learn and deepen our love for many more years.

Step 6: Fill yourself with passion for people and enjoy your life.

Earlier in the chapter I talked about my great grandfather Charles and my friend Edie. I remember Grandpa Charles having great passion for life. He was a rabbi and cantor, which meant he had a congregation, and in addition to doing sermons and helping the congregation he was involved with music, both singing and playing. He also had a passion for people. He seemed to know all the people in his congregation and told interesting stories about their lives.

Even as a small child I understood that he was a man who had a purpose in life. I knew he woke up every morning looking forward to the day. He was needed and he loved what he did. Helping others have a good life—physically, emotionally, and spiritually—was important to him. I remember thinking that when I grow up I want to be like Grandpa Charles.

But the thing that was really special about him for me was that he seemed to be committed to real, lasting love. I imagined that with his wives he was as passionate and caring with them as he was with his congregation. Growing up without a father, I never had the experience of a man who was committed to loving his partner.

Most of the "old people" I knew seemed to be pretty bland about their lives. There wasn't evidence of a lot of passion, either for their calling in life or for their love life. But Grandpa Charles seemed to have passion for it all.

When his wife died, he grieved her loss, but then he got back to living a full life. I didn't have to wonder how he found another partner to love. He exuded love that was evident to anyone, at any age. I still have a picture of him in his eighties with his sixty-something wife.

My friend Edie had a similar love of life and a desire to pair up with a loving partner, no matter at what age. When I was teaching a class, *Aging Well,* I invited her to come speak. She was ninety-nine at the time. I was concerned that I not tax her energy so I was trying to find a time that worked for her. The main concern she had wasn't her limited energy. It was finishing my class in time so she and her partner could go out dancing.

I asked her what the secrets of her long and active life were. She put dancing at the top of the list. "I love music and I love to dance. I also love to have a partner who holds me in his arms." In addition, she said she walked every day, loved to talk with people, and "I like to enjoy a glass of wine at the end of the day."

Another set of qualities that Edie had was that she was committed to "looking good" but was not afraid to appear foolish. I would often see her walking from her home to the bank. She was always dressed beautifully, often in a red dress, white gloves, and a classy hat. She didn't just look good for big celebrations. She dressed "to the nines" every day.

But Edie wasn't afraid to look foolish either. I still remember her in her late nineties at the local health club where I worked out regularly. She had come to swim and sit in the hot tub. To my surprise I saw her coming out of the locker room dressed only in a small towel. Edie isn't a big woman, but the skimpy club towel didn't fully cover her body.

When I approached and asked her what was going on, she smiled and told me, "I feel foolish. I can't seem to find my locker key." She didn't act like she felt foolish and she sure wasn't embarrassed. She needed help to find her key, and she wasn't going to sit helplessly in the locker room waiting for help to arrive.

I think of Charles and Edie as exemplifying a life that is three dimensional. They seemed to be living fully so that at the end they could answer these three questions in the affirmative:

1. Did I live my life authentically, true to my deepest self?
2. Did I love fully?
3. Did I make a difference in the life of others?

Why Is This Important? I think that being truly ourselves is a life-long journey and all three of these dimensions are inter-related. The more we can be ourselves, love ourselves, appreciate ourselves, enjoy ourselves—the more able we are to fully love another. And the more we are able to fully love others, the greater depth of love we have for ourselves. We might express this mathematically as 1 + 1 = Infinity. The power of a fully actualized one coming together with another can create magic that can change the world.

Step 7: Practice "The Seven Dances of Love."

Charles and Edie are great exemplars for me, but I'm often asked, "How do I get started? That treasure map you talked about seems to have so many dead-ends it's easy to get lost." People I counsel who are single and ready to move ahead to find a new love have lots of questions. Here are a few:

- I am not looking for a rich man to take care of me, but I do not want to partner with a man who is looking for someone to be a nurse and take care of him. How do I look for, locate, and find the person who is right for me?
- What the heck is going on in the dating world today? Does everybody hook up and have sex immediately?
- What if I am clear that I do not want to marry again but am interested in a committed relationship? How do I share that with a potential partner?
- What about dating sites? You hear so much about people being misled, cheated, etcetera. How can you be safe?
- If you have been deeply wounded by the end of a relationship, how do you know when you are ready to try again?

— What about alternative relationships? What if both people want to keep their own homes and finances, but want to be a "couple" for all other purposes?

Often the questions seem so overwhelming it's easy to stick with the life we've come to know. I've found that to find a new partner (or to revitalize a relationship with a partner you already have) it helps to practice what I call "The Seven Dances of Love." Like all sequences, not everyone takes them in order, but everyone who has worked with me on them has felt that these dances of life can help them find a partner, while taking their time to feel each advancing level of intimacy.

Before I share the seven dances with you, here's another exercise that will change the way you see yourself and how you might go about finding a mate. I often ask people in my workshops and counseling sessions to picture the ideal lover. How do they look, what do they do, how do they act, what are their best qualities? One man said I want a lover who is graceful, humorous, artistic, talented, and sexy. A woman wanted a lover who was successful, strong, romantic, and sensitive. When the person has their lover described in detail, I make the following suggestion. I'd like you to practice becoming the lover you hope to find.

To the man, for instance, I suggested he take a week and practice being graceful. Another week practice being humorous, and so on. For the woman, I suggested she practice being successful, strong, romantic, and sensitive.

I believe that each of us has all the potential to be whatever we want. If we become the lover we think we need, we won't feel so needy. We often seek out a partner, consciously or subconsciously, who has important qualities we think we lack. The more full and complete we feel, the more likely we are to find that special someone.

What are the qualities you are looking for in an ideal lover? How would your life be different if you possessed all those qualities? Go ahead and try living "as if" you already had that quality for a week and see how you feel.

Now let's explore "The Seven Dances of Love." People who engage these seven practices tell me that it allows them to move toward the kind of relationship they want at their own pace. It allows them to get to know others in a way that keeps them safe, before moving deeper into a new relationship. It also reminds us that each dance has its own reward. Too many of us become so bent on finding the ideal partner that we discount other ways of relating that may be valuable in and of themselves.

Dance #1: Acquaintanceship

The dance of acquaintanceship is to recognize that each person we meet is a gift from the universe. We see each person as a jewel to be appreciated without thought of whether they would be useful to us. Instead of screening out everyone except those few we think have "potential," we deeply appreciate everyone we meet.

When I was in college I had a friend named Jeanie. Jeanie was unusual in that she gave her full interest and attention to everyone she met. She just made you feel good to be alive.

Acquaintanceship acknowledges and enjoys each person simply because they are a fellow human being. Spend a week, or more, and practice giving your full attention and enjoyment on every person you meet. I sometimes imagine I'm Robinson Crusoe, stranded on a desert island and after many years finally see another human being. I would be overjoyed. I wouldn't care how tall they were, how pretty they were. I'd just be glad there was another human being in the world I could enjoy.

Dance #2: Companionship

The dance of companionship is to do what you love to do in the presence of other human beings. Singles out looking often tell me they go to places to meet people. Yet when I ask them if they enjoy the places they go and things they do, they acknowledge that they do not. "I just want to meet women and I was told this bar was a good place to do that. I go even though I hate bars."

If you want to see someone who truly understands the dance of companionship, watch a three-year-old playing in the sandbox with other children. He or she is ecstatic to be alive, to be playing in the sand, and to be with others of his kind.

In the dance of companionship, who is there is less important than abandoning oneself to the joy of doing. Try finding something you really enjoy and just do it wholeheartedly without worrying if you're finding that special someone.

Dance #3: Friendship

The dance of friendship combines being and doing. It is an interaction between two people who want to practice being themselves by doing things together with a partner. Where Dance #2 can be done with a number of partners, the dance of friendship comes in pairs.

We often think of friendship as a process of doing for the other person or having them do for us. It is really a process of being with another and enjoying getting closer to ourselves and to another.

Friendship is about getting to know ourselves and our partner. Most of us could use more friends, but when we're single we may be so focused on finding "Mr./Ms. Right" that we don't take time to make friends. Take your time. There's no hurry in this process. The worst that can happen if you stop at Dance #3 is that you'll have more friends.

Dance #4: Intimate Friendship

The dance of intimate friendship involves exploring the under-world. We begin to recognize in the other person things about ourselves that we don't like or accept. Intimate friends hold up a mirror to each other showing us what has been hidden and forbidden.

Intimate friends often go through times when they don't like each other very well or times when they are inseparable. The dance of intimate friendship is to reclaim lost parts of ourselves— to re-own our rage, terror, guilt, shame and also to reclaim our ability to appreciate, accept, nurture, and love ourselves.

Some people jump into intimacy too quickly. They share deeply intimate parts of their lives with someone they've only just met. It's as though they are afraid if someone really knew them they'd be rejected, so they jump in too quickly so they can get the rejection over with quickly. Others bail out at this stage, feeling there must be something wrong if they run into conflict with another person at this stage.

Intimate friendship is about learning to love and accept the "unacceptable" in ourselves and in the other person. It's worse hanging in there to really have the experience of intimacy.

Dance #5: Sensual Friendship

The dance of sensual friendship involves touching. Most of us are touch starved. We never got enough touching as infants, chil-dren, adolescents, and adults. Many of us rush into sex looking for the skin contact we never got.

Sensual friendship is not a prelude to sex. It is its own dance. In it we relearn to hold hands and rekindle the heat of touch-ing someone we have gotten to know intimately. We caress hair, shoulders, legs, buttocks, knees, and toes.

To learn sensual friendship we have to practice touching ourselves. Most of us rarely touch ourselves except when we are being sexual or when we are checking out our flaws. "Oh, I just can't do anything about my hair." Or, "My thighs are just too big." We pat, pinch, and poke ourselves, but rarely in a loving way.

In the dance of sensual friendship we touch ourselves and our partner simply for the pleasure that we receive and give.

Dance #6: Sexual/Creative Lovers

The dance of sexual/creative lovers recognizes that the purpose of sex is pleasure, creation, and bonding. As we have done with so much else in modern society, we often distill the process of sexuality and seek only the momentary pleasure.

For two million years of human history we sought out sexual partners for pleasure, but also to create children and develop the bond necessary to nurture and raise the children.

Those needs have not changed. Though we may not wish to create children each time we make love, the dance of sexual/creative lovers recognizes that creation is always involved in lovemaking. Each act of love creates a bond with our partner and has the potential to create new life—whether the life is a child, a poem, a dance, or an affirmation of the rebirth of the spirit.

The dance of sexual/creative lovers continually renews our commitment to life. Think of each sexual act as having the potential of being a beautiful and unique "love child" into the world. Each sexual encounter is truly an act of creation.

Dance #7: Spiritual/Life Partners

The dance of spiritual/life partners recognizes that we cannot truly commit to be with a partner for the rest of our lives until we have gone through the other stages. It knows that the goal of spiritual/life partnership is not happiness, but the spiritual development of each of the partners and the growth of the partnership itself.

In this dance we develop the comfort and security of knowing that the partnership is being held in the embrace of a spiritual presence that teaches each partner how to express and receive ever deeper experiences of joy and ecstasy.

Which dances are most familiar to you? Which ones are least familiar? Where have you gotten stuck in the past? With which dances do you need more practice to become an expert?

For most of us who have been raised on a diet of "instant intimacy," "The Seven Dances of Love" seem slow, cumbersome, and old-fashioned. The only thing they have to recommend them is that they work.

If you are open to practicing them, I offer the following suggestions:

1. Pursue each dance for its own value. When you're practicing "Companionship," for instance, take the attitude that if you died tomorrow and had only learned to be an excellent companion, life would be worthwhile.

2. Enjoy each dance without planning the next. "Intimate Friendship" and "Sensual Friendship," for instance, are not "foreplay" for sex. Each is the main event.

3. Don't let someone else's needs change the dance you want to practice. If someone wants you to join the "Sexual/Creative Lovers" dance, for instance, but you want to practice "Intimate Friendship," stand up for your own needs.

4. Even if you are already in a relationship, it's wonderful to go back and start over. Take a week and practice acquaintanceship, for instance. Look at your partner through new eyes as a wonderful, unique gift from

God without any agenda for where the relationship
might go in the future.

Why Is This Important? It seems to be one of those facts of life
that when we go after something directly we often push it further away. When we go looking for "the love of our lives," we create so much hope and fear and we get in our own way. However,
when we take our mind off the "goal" and just enjoy each dance
for its own sake, we often find that special someone is just there,
unexpectedly.

In the next chapter I'll introduce you to a number of couples
who are using the Power of Two to extend their love out in the
world to make a difference for all people.

Twelve

You Two Can Change the World: If Not You, Who? If Not Now, When?

Sigmund Freud said "Love and work are the cornerstones to our humanness." Just as love goes through multiple stages, so too does our work. Early in our lives, we worked in order to make a living. When we started out, we took whatever job we could find in order to make enough money to support ourselves and our families. Later, if we were lucky, we found a career that gave us the satisfaction of an ongoing commitment to our craft. But later in life our focus shifts from our *career* to our *calling*. We want our work to have deeper meaning and to make a difference in the world. We often want to be mentors and share what we've learned with others.

Psychologist Abraham Maslow talked about "self-actualization" as being the pinnacle of the human needs pyramid. The term was originally introduced by the theorist Kurt Goldstein for the desire to realize one's full potential. This would often express itself through our creative outlets, our quest for spiritual enlightenment, and the desire to give back to society. Though there was a focus outward to the larger world, it was still seen as something that an individual did. It became the ultimate expression of our personal life path.

However, I've come to see that one of the true benefits of moving through the five stages of love and marriage as a couple allows us to engage the fifth stage—Finding Your Calling as a Couple. In stage 5 we can begin to use the Power of Two to focus our attention outwards to address issues in the larger world that needed to be fixed. Instead of thinking about "self-actualization" or "finding our calling" as an individual, I'm suggesting that we think about what we can do as a couple to change the world.

It's clear to more and more people that our present focus on continued consumption of the earth's resources is not sustainable. We are coming to see that we are living on a finite planet and infinite growth is impossible. Things must change if we are going to survive as a species. Millions of species have become extinct since life first evolved on earth. *Homo sapiens* certainly could join the departed if we don't change our ways.

John L. Petersen, president and founder of the prestigious Arlington Institute, is considered by many to be one of the most informed futurists in the world. In 2012 he warned, "Converging trends strongly suggest that the world—and our country—are about to experience the greatest change and disruption known in our history. The next half dozen years will likely see rapid, global climate change coupled with the beginning of the end of the petroleum era and a reorganization of the planetary energy regime, a major shock to the global financial system, unprecedented food prices, and the growing possibility of wild card events."[1] These are events such as the wildfires that raged through northern California, Hurricane Katrina that devastated the Gulf Coast, or the killings in Paris, which could not be specifically predicted, but are the likely result of humanity out of balance with nature.

These life-changing events remind me of the film *Koyaanisqatsi: Life Out of Balance*, a 1982 documentary directed by Godfrey Reggio, with music composed by Philip Glass and cinematography by Ron Fricke. There was no dialogue in the film, just images and hauntingly beautiful music. According to Hopi Dictionary, *Hopìikwa Lavàytutuveni*, the Hopi word *koyaanisqatsi* (Hopi pronunciation: koja:nis'katsi) is defined as "life of moral corruption and turmoil" or "life out of balance."

In her book *The Watchman's Rattle: A Radical New Theory of Collapse*, Rebecca Costa offers an in-depth understanding of the underlying causes of this imbalance. She recognizes the complexity is making it difficult for humans to solve the problems we have created in the world.

Clearly, if human beings are going to survive as a species, we must heal our connection to the earth. We must also heal our connection to ourselves and each other. I believe that couples are being called to this larger purpose. As our love expands outward we want to work together to help us save our children, grandchildren, and all future generations. Let me be clear: I'm not suggesting that every couple has to find a big issue that they tackle together. I'm not even suggesting that there is a single issue that both members of the couple will take on together. I am saying that as we get into our forties, fifties, and sixties, we begin to feel called to address larger issues in the world. These issues may be an extension of our work, either paid or volunteer, or they may be something that has been in the background of our lives and is now coming to the fore.

One person may take the lead on an issue and the other person may remain more in the background providing support. We may be the leader on one issue and the support person on another. Or there may be an issue that both members of the partnership want to address. We may each bring our unique perspective and skills to the problem.

I'd like to introduce you to a number of couples who are engaged in making a positive difference in the world. I hope their efforts will inspire other couples to engage more fully and share their own efforts to make the world a better place for all.

Growing Soil to Feed the World: John and Cynthia Raiser Jeavons

John Jeavons is literally a man of the earth. Without the precious earth we cannot grow food to feed people. He reminds us that

> "Six inches of farmable soil is needed to grow food and other crops. In Nature, soil genesis takes an average of 500 years on the Earth to grow one inch of this wonderful element. This means it takes 3,000 years to grow six inches."
>
> Globally, our present farming practices are depleting soil 18 to 80 times faster than it is built in nature, John says. "6 to 24 pounds (depending on the world region) of farmable soil are lost per pound of food eaten due to wind and water erosion fostered by conventional farming practices. Some studies even indicate that as little as 30 to 40 years of farmable soil may remain on the planet. Most people soon will have only 4,500 square feet per person on which to grow their sustenance."[2]

The consequences of our present practices are devastating. Here are a few examples cited by John:

- Fifty percent of Africa is already on starvation track.
- Fifty percent of the people living in Mexico are spending 70 percent of their disposable income on food since 2013—only getting one-third of their calories each day.
- The UN-FAO indicates that in ten years two-thirds of the world population—5.5 billion people—may

not have enough water to grow a sufficient diet,
and many of them will have no food at all.[3] John's
approach of *biologically intensive* food growing can
grow sufficient food for a complete diet annually on
as little as 1,000 square feet with 33 percent the water,
while—if used properly—*growing soil* up to 60 times
faster than in Nature—6 inches in as little as fifty
years. During this build-up time, food and compost
materials can be produced as well.

Says John, "Aware of intensifying world challenges and the
basic need of people to feed themselves, we have been working for 40 years to develop an elegant, small-scale agricultural
system—GROW BIOINTENSIVE® Sustainable Mini-Farming—
that when practiced correctly, nurtures healthy soil fertility,
produces high yields, conserves resources and can be used successfully by almost everyone. Our goal is to help this system be
known and used locally . . . on a worldwide basis."[4] This method
is now being used successfully by millions of people in 151 countries in virtually all soils and climates where food is grown.

Although John is the public face of this important movement,
his wife, Cynthia, is an integral part of the team. I often see her
at talks and trainings answering questions, taking pictures, and
offering physical and emotional support. John and Cynthia met
in 1987 and were married in 1995. Says John, "Cynthia has pro-
vided constant moral, logistical, conceptual and political support."[5] Cynthia is a professional photographer and many of the
images on their website have been taken by her.

Their daughter, Rose, born in 1999, often works in the gar-
den alongside her parents and engages with the students who
come from around the world to the farm and training facility
in Willits. When I asked John what's the most important thing
that is needed in the world, his answer was simple: "We need to
GROW SOIL now. It is the basis upon which all life depends."[6]

You can learn more about the Jeavons' work here: *www.growbiointensive.org/* and *http://cynthiaraiserjeavons.zenfolio .com/*.

Couple Counseling and Chatting—An App for Our Times: Marigrace Randazzo-Ratliff and Dustin Ratliff

Many people are using technology to find a partner. Sites like Match.com, eHarmony.com, and Chemistry.com help people find that special someone. But most of us find that, difficult as it is to find a mate, it is even more difficult to keep a relationship alive and well. Marigrace Randazzo-Ratliff, who has been a therapist since 1988, felt that technology could help couples. We've all heard the saying "We've got an app for that," but is there really an app that would help couples communicate more effectively? Marigrace thought there should be and decided to develop one.

"I believe people are mostly stuck, not sick or crazy," says Marigrace. "I also feel that it is darn hard to be vulnerable as a client and talk about one's struggles and mistakes. I let my clients know we are a team working together to turn their life around. I also tell them if they want their lives to change they better work their asses off."

Marigrace's work was featured in a March 2014 article in the *New York Times.* Writer Abby Ellin began the article: "Here is what Steve S. and Sarah B. do when they fight: They take a breath, go to their smartphones, and click on Couples Counseling & Chatting, a free app created by their real-life therapist, Marigrace Randazzo-Ratliff."[7]

In describing her innovative way to help people, Marigrace says, "The app has been an international success because it was really the first-ever to leverage the smart phone capabilities to be more than an electronic book or personality test. The app helps couples become self-aware, understand one another, communicate and connect. The app teaches that men connect with their emotions differently and as a result I have more male users of my app than female, which I believe is a first in the field of psychology. Men from all over the world want to improve their relationships, and they seem to be more receptive to tools like apps than 1:1 therapy or books. I know if I can help these men with their marriages, they will become great role models for their boys. I plan to have many more apps, including one for teenagers to help keep them safe and get them out of difficult situations, like when they are exposed to drugs, sex, or problems at home."[8]

Marigrace and Dustin met in October 1995 while volunteering at the Ann Arbor Civic Theater. Dustin was tech director and Marigrace was a co-producer. They married two years later and have two children, a boy and a girl. Looking back over the years together, Dustin reflects on their similarities and differences. "While Marigrace and I have very similar interests, values, work ethics, life goals, etc., she and I communicate very differently. And in many ways we see the world very differently."[9]

"It took a long time to figure out those communication differences. Like most couples with stereotypical male/female individuals, Marigrace is very good with words and connecting emotionally. She's an expert at it really, given how hard she had to work at trying to fix her close family relationships, or form meaningful external ones in order to survive. I on the other hand, while not your typical male in terms of following sports or downing several beers with my buddies every Saturday, have the typical difficulties with connecting with or articulating my feelings, focusing on tasks and finances rather than another person's feelings, and getting easily defensive or disconnected when addressing something I've done incorrectly or failed to do."

These similarities and differences have enabled them to form a good team in bringing the Couples Counseling and Chatting app to the world. Dustin describes some of the difficulties he has had being in the supportive role while Marigrace was the leader in developing and getting the couples app out to the public. "I was pulled in to help type, translate, and structure Marigrace's information to fit into the workings of the app. It proved to be a very difficult process as a couple. We really needed to learn how to collaborate on something, or maybe more specifically, I needed to learn how to take direction and remain focused on the creator's vision and direction without going off on what I thought should be done."

Says Marigrace, "We are both very concerned about the way society is going and we are both dedicated to putting out great tools to help people deal with what they're facing today. I am so blessed and fortunate to have a spouse who works with me and shares the same desires for change. My husband is the CFO and COO in my company Psyched by MG, LLC and he has his own plans to create apps of his own in the future."

You can learn more about the Randazzo-Ratliff work here: *www.Psychedbymg.com/.*

Helping Men Survive and Thrive: Stephen and Fran Johnson

"As I was going through the darkest part of my mid-life crisis," says Stephen Johnson, "I was given a revelation to focus my attention on serving men and improving the plight of men and their many issues often centered on what I refer to as *The Father Gap.*" Dr. Johnson, a psychotherapist in practice since 1970, went on to develop the first *Sacred Path Men's Retreats* in 1987 and the following year founded the Men's Center of Los Angeles.

Over the years the Men's Center has facilitated numerous workshops and over one hundred *Sacred Path Men's Retreats* and *Call to Adventure Rites of Passage Retreats* for fathers and sons, young males and mentors. "We're in our 28th year of service to the men's community," says Stephen. "Our mission statement is: Bringing Good Men Together to Bring Out the Best in Them." Johnson's experiences and learnings are well presented in his book, *The Sacred Path: The Way of the Spiritual Warrior; Journey to Mindful Manhood.*

Ritual elder Malidoma Patrice Somé says, "Elders and mentors have an irreplaceable function in the life of any community. Without them the young are lost—their overflowing energies wasted in useless pursuits. In the absence of the elders, the impetuosity of youth becomes the slow death of the community."[10] The work of Dr. Johnson is particularly important in bringing older males together with younger males so that young men can get the nurturing and support they so desperately need.

I attended one of the retreats along with my grandsons, Deon and Derrick, and their father, Walter. There were more than forty boys, many from poor, inner-city neighborhoods, who attended the four-day retreat. Some of the most powerful experiences occurred when we met in small tribal groups facilitated by trained leaders and attended by eight to ten boys and their mentors. We went around the circle and talked about why we were here. My grandson Deon opened up immediately and told the group, "I'm lost in my life and I need guidance."

Young and old knew what he meant and many shared their own feelings of being lost. For the first time I had a deep experience of the violence that so many of these kids live with every day. One boy talked about killings he had seen in his neighborhood, and Deon also talked about people he knew who had been murdered. Another young boy said that didn't want a lot in life, just to know that he would survive another day.

At the end of the retreat Stephen addressed the group. "Our boys, young men, and our mature men are calling on us to explore with clarity what the role of fathers, grandfathers, and mentors should be. If we do not provide a sacred role for our boys as they grow, they are more likely to join a gang, abuse their lovers, abandon their wives and children, subsist in emotional isolation, and become addicted, hyper-materialistic, lonely, and unhappy."

Stephen and his wife, Fran, have faced challenges in their own family."[11] Diving into motherhood was fairly difficult and created a type of isolation that I hadn't ever experienced before," says Fran. "While Steve worked non-stop I was suddenly moved to the San Fernando Valley, a place many have thought is a proper wasteland. I had moved to California from New York City where I had a promising career as an actor. The marriages of our parents' generation were both very traditional so it seemed appropriate for us to have the same."

"I wasn't prepared for the load I carried," Fran remembers, "and I know he wasn't prepared for his load of long hours at work. Thus, we seemed to move along on separate paths while trying to achieve the same goal: a stable, healthy and happy family. I believe it caused a certain amount of isolation on both our parts. It was tough but we soldiered on."

Stephen continues looking back at the challenges of family life. "The first major challenge we faced was about six years into our relationship when our daughter, Dana, was born prematurely at twenty-six weeks, weighing less than a pound and a half. We had two sons, a four-year-old and a 10-month-old, at home at the time that our daughter was in the neonatal critical care unit for six months and then came home on a sleep apnea monitor that would sound a 90-decibel alarm each time she stopped breathing. The alarm could go off several times a night. She was on it for one and a half years."

"I'm happy to report that Dana just celebrated her thirty-first birthday," Stephen told me, "defying the less-than-10-percent odds of survival. "Instead of being a victim of her personal challenges she has become a victor over adversity."

"Another challenge for our relationship has been the chronic and often acute health conditions that have plagued my wife, essentially since I've known her during the past thirty-eight years. On the lighter side, I've quipped, 'Maybe I've been bad luck for you.' On the heavier side, residing with someone who has ongoing health issues does tend to put a crimp in your own lifestyle. At times it hasn't brought out the best in me but I've endeavored to allow this particular challenge to teach me how to be a more enduring, tolerant, patient, compassionate and loving man. I'm still on a learning curve that I trust will continue on the incline."

"I am often asked by younger women about my relationship with my husband," says Fran "I always say, 'Long term relationships are cyclical. One day you're planning what you will wear to his funeral and the next you're planning a sexy weekend away.' I think it's important to have friends of all ages because you always teach and learn at the same time."

"For me, because I do not have a large platform, communicating with people on a personal basis is the most rewarding way I can give to our world," Fran concludes. "Everyone has a 'ministry,' whether it's feeding the homeless, teaching kindness, helping our neighbors in need or just being the person who plans a birthday party for co-workers. It's an opportunity to spread goodness and love."

You can learn more about Stephen's work here: *www.menscenterlosangeles.com.*

Improving Male Health and Well-Being: Greg Millan and Richard Riley

Greg Millan and Richard Riley are passionate about men's health. Greg is a social work trained health educator with over twenty-seven years of experience promoting men's health. Richard is also a social worker who has been helping people with HIV for more than twenty years.

Greg is the vice president of the Australian Men's Health Forum, the country's primary organization for implementing a social approach to male health. He is also a member of the International Society for Men's Health (ISMH), and a member of the Board of Advisors of the Men's Health Network USA and Toronto Men's Health Network, Canada.

Richard says, "As a social worker I work with not only the individual but with those areas that impact on the person's experience. So there is often work to do with friends, partners, family, the health system, employers, service providers within and outside the HIV field and in the areas of counseling, practical assistance, advocacy, consultation, service and policy development. The social construction of HIV is often very different to how a HIV positive person perceives their life. Living with that disconnection requires a set of skills that I hope to help people with. I'd also like to change and improve the social construct itself."

Greg's book, *Men's Health & Wellbeing: An A–Z Guide,* has been lauded by those working in the field of men's health worldwide. Psychologist Peter West says, "The old script for men was simple. Perform, protect, provide. That meant, work hard, most of your life. Protect your loved ones, and usually that meant your wife and children. And provide food, clothing and shelter for them. If they could get some time off, men would play sport, go to the pub, and grab what sex they could."[12] West says that Greg's book offers a more comprehensive view of what constitutes manhood and what men really need to do well in life.

Greg and Richard first met in 1979, but began dating seriously in June 1990 and have been in a relationship for more than twenty-five years. They were married in New Zealand on

September 15, 2013, where same-sex marriages had just become legal. Greg says that it's been difficult living in a country that doesn't support the values and rights of all its people.

"It isn't easy being a gay male couple as society still makes life difficult or assumes that all people are heterosexual and therefore anyone who is not is the 'other' and in some way different," says Greg. "We all have so much in common, but issues like gay marriage, bring out arguments against the basic human rights of gay, lesbian, gay, bi, trans and intersex (LGBTI) people. We are not happy we live in a country that has not recognized gay marriage."

"When we married in New Zealand two years ago," says Greg, "it was a total game changer to see our families and friends and workmates reacting with such love, support and generosity. It makes us feel more whole and more a part of a world that acknowledges and respects our relationship, that sees the love regardless of their sexual orientation."[13]

Richard and Greg also face challenges that all couples must deal with when one has a serious health problem. "Greg's battle with leukemia during 2006 through 2009 was a time that revealed his strength and great attitude to managing very difficult times," Richard recalls. "We took it on, one peak and trough at a time, on what was a roller coaster of emotions. There was the threat of death if a donor couldn't be found or if the transplant was rejected. There was the debilitation caused by the illness and the treatment.

"We tangled roles of career and caretaking. We had to learn to cope with being cared for and being a caregiver, along with our roles as independent people as lovers and friends. We accepted love and support from others but realized it was we two that had to work it out and do what we had to do. We found we were learning new things about each other. We found that we could rely on each other in the worst of times."

Their experiences with career and caring have brought them closer together and more caring of others. "We need to be more compassionate to others in the world," they say. "We only have one life and one place to spend that life, so we need to be compassionate and caring for others, for animals, and for the planet so that future generations can live in peace and prosper."

You can learn more about Greg's work here: *www.mens healthservices.com.au.*

Health, Aging, and the Inner Journey: Barbara and Ernie Hubbard

Barbara and Ernie Hubbard are an unusual couple. They have been together for twenty-three years and Barbara is twenty-three years older than Ernie. I asked them about challenges they have faced that have strengthened their marriage. Says Barbara, "I'm the female in this otherwise-unconventional marriage. I am older than my husband by more than twenty years. I don't have an explanation as to why it works so well, except I just never worried about age and neither does he."

Ernie tells me, "Ours is an unconventional marriage in a number of respects, but at the core it is everything I could have ever hoped for. Clearly, this is a lifelong process of growth and learning. We are becoming one." Both Ernie and Barbara have been married before, and their past has infused their present with wisdom and joy.

Ernie was born in the San Francisco Bay area, in Marin County. "I spent most of my youth along the banks of the Sacramento River in the small town of Colusa," he told me. "My father was a country lawyer and most of my friends were involved in agriculture." Ernie is a scientist and has kept the love of biology he first encountered growing up on a farm. He pursued graduate studies in molecular and cell biology at the University of Minnesota. He is now the cofounder, along with physician/biochemist Michael Rosenbaum, MD, of the Sage Center, which focuses on healthy aging, safe food, and natural beauty.

I suspect that some of Ernie's interest in natural beauty comes from his wife, Barbara, who is quite beautiful as she approaches her ninetieth birthday in August 2016. Barbara was a model earlier in her life as well as a professional dancer. In recent years she has authored a number of books and is planning a book on weight loss based on her own experiences.

When I visited with Ernie and Barbara recently, they were both recovering from the effects of a fall Barbara had taken a number of months previously and the various medical interventions they had tried to help her recover full function. She was doing quite well, moving around more easily, and even trying out some of her dance steps.

Looking ahead, they are both committed to supporting each other as they age and addressing the changes going on in the world. "I'm most concerned about the effect of human nature upon the Cosmos and the general lack of awareness of this," says Ernie. "We may have passed the tipping point where we can get back in balance with nature without a major loss of human life."

Although Ernie has spent decades helping to bring about changes in the outer world, he says that the changes he's involved with now are more internal. "It is almost exclusively a non-physical process, and I believe it may be of help to others by helping me mature and be in a position to serve those in need." I found that a very hopeful and realistic approach to addressing the huge changes going on in the world. Sometimes we have to deal with "non-physical processes," as Ernie describes them. We may need more people who marshal their inner resources and make themselves available to be of service to others during these times of unprecedented change.

Ernie and Barbara are giving a lot of support to each other. "Barbara has always supported my journey, as my life partner, friend, advisor, confidant, co-traveler and more," says Ernie. "In short, she believes in me. I hope I reciprocate, supporting her emotionally, physically, financially, technically, and spiritually."

You can get more information about Ernie's work here: http://www.erniehubbard.org/

Disease Proofing Our Lives: David and Catherine Katz

According to David Katz, MD, who we first met in Chapter 10, "Heart disease *is not* the leading cause of death among men and women in the United States. Cancer, stroke, pulmonary disease, diabetes, and dementia *are not* the other leading causes of early mortality and/or chronic malady either."[14] I was startled when I first read these words by Dr. Katz, who is one of the world's leading experts on health and disease. But he went on to clarify these statements. "Don't get me wrong—these *are* the very diseases immediately responsible for an enormous loss of years from life, and an even greater loss of life from years. In that context, heart disease is indeed the most common immediate precipitant of early death among women and men alike. Cancer, stroke, and diabetes do indeed follow close behind. It's just that these diseases aren't really causes. They are effects."

As founder of the True Health Initiative (*http://lifestyle medicine.org/True-Health-Initiative)*, Dr. Katz is convening a global coalition of the world's leading authorities and organizations in health-related fields (e.g., lifestyle medicine, preventive medicine, public health, health journalism, environmentalism, sustainable agriculture, conservation, nutrition, health care, etc.). "Imagine a global voice devoted to—and only to—disseminating and applying what we know for sure about health promotion and disease prevention so authoritative, that everyone stops to listen," says Dr. Katz. "Imagine that singularly authoritative voice establishing for chronic disease prevention a mandate as clear and actionable as the campaign that led to the global eradication of smallpox."

In his book *Disease Proof: The Remarkable Truth About What Makes Us Well*, Dr. Katz details the ways we can take charge of our health. He gives us the science, but also the secrets of putting the science into action so that we can all live well throughout our lives. When asked why he wrote the book, Dr. Katz says that the book provides an honest, comprehensive, and empowering dose of the skills required to lose weight and find health. "It really can help add years to lives, and life to years, and I would like your life and your family to be among the beneficiaries. Why? It's probably selfish. I'm one of those people who has to do good, or at least try my best, to feel good about myself. If I can make a positive difference in the world, my life is better. I admit that's selfish, but I think it's a good kind of selfish. I want to help people get to health, and in doing so, I help myself to a feeling a fulfillment. Everybody wins."[15]

For David Katz, this commitment to health found new meaning when he met his wife, Catherine, in 1991 at an epidemiology class Catherine was auditing at Yale. David was an aspiring preventive medicine resident. Catherine describes herself as a French-born-and-raised foodie, and lover of luscious cuisine. But she's also a scientist with a PhD in neuroscience from Princeton University.

Catherine remembers how their interests and experience came together around food. "When David presented me with the challenge of his very demanding nutrition standards, we realized that his passion for health and my love of French cooking also needed to be wed! And so our 'marriage' of priorities resulted in 20 some years of methodical experimentation—but in our warm, lively home kitchen, rather than any neuroscience lab. Over those years, David and I have raised 5 beautiful healthy children together—Rebecca, Corinda, Valerie, Natalia and Gabe (I stopped working as a neuroscientist after Natalia was born)— and all of us have benefited from our shared passion for loving food that loves us back."[16]

David reflects back on some of the challenges he has faced over the years trying to get establishment medicine to have a more enlightened view of nutrition and health. "In the world of work and strife, I have faced some considerable battles, some of which were a threat to livelihood and career. When there was a choice between security and integrity, we chose integrity together and put our security at risk to support one another in doing what we believed to be right. That has always been our modus operandi, and we have always been stronger for embracing it together. And, it has always worked out over time, but it has also often been quite scary at the time!"[17]

David, Catherine, and their family remain dedicated to helping us all become healthier and happier. "We work directly together on projects, books, and websites," they told me. "But the more important element is that we share the emotional aspects of living through every endeavor. When it's hard, we are one another's sanctuary of understanding, support, and comfort. When it is wonderful, it is more wonderful because we can share it with one another. When it is tense and suspenseful, we suffer through the waiting together. When it is disappointing, we are still together and so know that it will be OK. In unity, there is strength to succeed, and to suffer failures and try again. We are one another's unity; we are one another's strength."

You can learn more about Dr. Katz's work here: *www.davidkatzmd.com/*; and access Catherine's wonderful recipes here: *http://cuisinicity.com/*

Think about your own future. What do you see in the world that needs doing? What can you do in partnership that would make your efforts more fun and more successful? Sharing this book with you has been a joy. Although I may be the lead author, you can be sure that everything I've done, including this book, has Carlin's loving fingerprints all over it. I look forward to connecting with you and hearing about your own journey.

NOTES

Chapter 1

1. Helen Fisher, *Why We Love: The Nature and Chemistry of Romantic Love.* New York: Henry Holt and Company, 78, and personal correspondence June 23, 2015.

Chapter 2

1. Joshua Wolf Shenk, *Powers of Two: How Relationships Drive Creativity,* New York: Houghton Mifflin Harcourt, 2014, xi.
2. Michael Gurian, *Lessons of Lifelong Intimacy: Building a Stronger Marriage Without Losing Yourself,* New York: Atria Books, 2015, 5.
3. Esther Perel, *Mating in Captivity: Reconciling the Erotic & the Domestic,* New York: HarperCollins, 2006, xv.
4. Kahlil Gibran, *The Prophet,* New York: Alfred A. Knopf, 1923.
5. Michael Dowd, *Thank God for Evolution: How the Marriage of Science and Religion Will Transform Your Life and Our World,* New York: Penguin, 2009, 148.
6. Ibid.
7. Ibid, 150.
8. Elkhonon Goldberg, *The Executive Brain: Frontal Lobes and the Civilized Mind,* Oxford, U.K.: Oxford University Press, 2009, 2.
9. Michael Dowd, *Thank God for Evolution: How the Marriage of Science and Religion Will Transform Your Life and Our World,* New York: Penguin, 2009, 152.
10. John Gottman and Nan Silver, *What Makes Love Last? How to build trust and avoid betrayal,* New York: Simon & Schuster, 2012, xvii.
11. Gerald G. Jampolsky, *Love is Letting Go of Fear,* New York: Celestial Arts, 1979, 2011, 8.

Chapter 3

1. James R. Doty, MD, *Into the Magic Shop: A Neurosurgeon's Quest to Discover the Mysteries of the Brain and the Secrets of the Heart*, New York: Avery, 2016.
2. John Gottman and Nan Silver, *What Makes Love Last? How to build trust and avoid betrayal*, New York: Simon & Schuster, 2012, xvii-xviii.
3. Donna Jackson Nakazawa, *Childhood Disrupted: How Your Biography Becomes Your Biology, and How You Can Heal*, New York: Atria Books, 2015.
4. Bessel Van Der Kolk, MD, *The Body Keeps the Score: Brain, Mind, and Body in the Healing of Trauma* (New York: Viking, 2014), 1.
5. Donna Jackson Nakazawa, *Childhood Disrupted: How Your Biography Becomes Your Biology, and How You Can Heal*, New York: Atria Books, 2015, 37.
6. Ibid, 96.
7. Ibid, 96.
8. Mario Martinez, *The Mind Body Code: How to Change the Beliefs that Limit your Health, Longevity, and Success*, Boulder, Colorado: Sounds True, 2014, 21.
9. Ibid, 36.

Chapter 4

1. Joseph Campbell, *Pathways to Bliss: Mythology and Personal Transformation*, Novato, California: New World Library, 2004, quoted by Maria Popova, *www.brainpickings.org/2015/06/29/pathways-to-bliss -joseph-campbell-marriage-relationships/*
2. Angeles Arrien, Living in Gratitude: *Mastering the Art of Giving Thanks Every Day*, Boulder, Colorado: Sounds True, 2013, 167.
3. Jed Diamond, "Saving Your Midlife Marriage, Even if Only One of You is Trying to Keep it Alive." MenAlive, November 15, 2013, *http:// menalive.com/5-secrets-for-saving-your-mid-life-marriage-even-when-only -one-of-you-is-trying-to-keep-it-alive/*
4. Thomas Merton, *No Man is an Island. www.goodreads.com/author/quotes /1711.Thomas_Merton*

Chapter 5

1. Marianne J. Legato, M.D., *Eve's Rib: The New Science of Gender-Specific Medicine and How It Can Save Your Life*, New York: Harmony Books, 2002, xi.
2. David C. Page, M.D. "TEDX talk." *www.youtube.com/watch?v=n QcgD5DpVlQ*
3. Ibid.

4. Larry Cahill. "Drugs Can Affect Men and Women Differently." CBS News, *60 Minutes*, *www.cbsnews.com/news/drugs-can-affect-men-and -women-differently/*
5. Ibid.
6. Marianne J. Legato, *Why Men Never Remember and Women Never Forget*, Emmaus, PA: Rodale, 2005, xiv.
7. David C. Page, M.D. "TEDX talk." *www.youtube.com/watch?v=n QcgD5DpVlQ*
8. Marianne J. Legato, *Why Men Never Remember and Women Never Forget*, Emmaus, PA: Rodale, 2005, 68-69.
9. Louann Brizendine, M.D., *The Female Brain*, New York: Morgan Road Books, 2006, xvii.
10. Theresa L. Crenshaw, *The Alchemy of Love and Lust: How Our Sex Hormones Influence Our Relationships*, New York: Gallery Books, 1997, p. 5, and personal correspondence.
11. Paul J. Zak, *The Moral Molecule: The Source of Love and Prosperity*, New York: Dutton, 2012, xii.
12. Simon Baron-Cohen, *The Essential Difference: The Truth about the Male & Female Brain*, New York: Basic Books, 2003, 1.

Chapter 6

1. John L. Locke, *Duels and Duets: Why Man and Women Talk So Differently*, Cambridge: Cambridge University Press, 2011, 4.
2. Ibid.
3. Ibid, 7.
4. Deborah Tennen, *You Just Don't Understand: Women and Men in Conversation*, New York, Quill, 1990, 77
5. Laura A. Munson, "Those Aren't Fighting Words, Dear," The New York Times, July 31, 2009, *www.nytimes.com/2009/08/02/fashion/02lone .html?_r=0*
6. Jed Diamond, "It Takes One to Tango: How You Can Save Your Relationship, Even if Your Partner Wants to Leave, " MenAlive, *http:// menalive.com/it-takes-one-to-tango/*
7. Amy Sutherland, *What Shamu Taught Me about Life, Love, and Marriage*, New York: Random House, 2008, 9.
8. Ibid, 12.
9. Ibid, 13.
10. Patricia Love and Steven Stosny, *How to Improve Your Marriage Without Talking About It*, New York: Broadway Books, 2007, 1-2.

Chapter 7

1. Kay Redfield Jamison. *An Unquiet Mind: Memoir of Moods and Madness*, New York: Vintage Books, 1995, 218.

2. Andrew Oswald and David Blanchflower, "Researchers Find That Middle-Aged Misery Spans the Globe," *www2.warwick.ac.uk/news andevents/pressreleases/researchers_find_that/*

3. Ibid.

4. Jed Diamond, *The Irritable Male Syndrome: Managing the 4 Key Causes of Depression and Aggression,* Emmaus, Pa: Rodale, 2004, 82.

5. J. Douglas Bremner, M.D., *Does Stress Damage the Brain? Understanding Trauma-Related Disorders from a Mind-Body Perspective,* New York: W.W. Norton, 2005. Personal correspondence.

6. Will Courtenay, *Dying to Be Men: Psychosocial, Environmental, and Biobehavioral Directions in Promoting the Health of Men and Boys* New York: Routledge, 2011, 6.

7. John T. Cacioppo & William Patrick, *Loneliness: Human Nature and the Need for Social Connection,* New York: W.W. Norton, 2008, 5.

8. Thomas Joiner, *Lonely at the Top: The High Cost of Men's Success,* New York: Palgrave Macmillan, 2011, 12.

9. Ibid.

10. Ibid, 13

11. Carlin Diamond, *Love It, Don't Label It: A Practical Guide for Using Spiritual Principles in Everyday Life,* San Rafael, California: Fifth Wave Press, 1985, x.

12. Andrew Solomon, *The Noonday Demon: An Atlas of Depression,* New York: Scribner, 2001, 15.

13. United Nations Global Environmental Outlook, *www.unep.org/geo/*

Chapter 8

1. Gail Sheehy, "The Unspeakable Passage. Is There a Male Menopause?" *Vanity Fair,* April, 1993, 164+.

2. Lisa Jey Davis, *Getting Over Your Ovaries: How to Make 'The Change of Life' Your Bitch.* To be published, 2016-2017. *http://lisajeydavis.com/books /getting-over-your-ovaries/*

3. Jonathan V. Wright, M.D. and Lane Lenard. *Maximize Your Vitality and Potency: For Men Over 40.* Petaluma, California: Smart Publications, 1999). Personal communication.

4. Jed Diamond, *Surviving Male Menopause: A Guide for Women and Men* (Naperville, Ill: Sourcebooks, 2000), 4-5.

5. Paul De Kruif, *The Male Hormone,* New York: Permabooks, 1948, 50.

6. Charles Patrick Davis, M.D., Ph.D., "High and Low Testosterone in Men." *www.medicinenet.com/high_and_low_testosterone_levels_in_men /views.htm*

7. James McBride Dabbs, *Heroes, Rogues, and Lovers: Testosterone and Behavior,* New York: McGraw-Hill, 2000, 163.

8. Ibid.

9. Ibid.
10. Ibid, 165.

Chapter 9

1. Susan Faludi, *Stiffed: The Betrayal of the American Man*, New York: William Morrow, 1999. Personal correspondence.
2. Ibid.
3. Boadie W. Dunlop, M.D., "Depressing Future for Men," *British Journal of Psychiatry*, March 11, 2011, 167-168.
4. Rick Marin. "Dead Suit Walking: Can Manhood Survive the Recession?" *Newsweek*, April 11, 2011.
5. Václav Havel, "The Need for Transcendence in the Postmodern World." Speech, Independence Hall, Philadelphia, on July 4, 1994. *www.worldtrans.org/whole/havelspeech.html*
6. Rob Watson. "The End of Men and the Rise of Women, Or Are We Facing The End of Us All?" *http://goodmenproject.com/featured-content/cc-the-end-of-men-and-the-rise-of-women-or-are-we-facing the end-of-us-all/*
7. Daniel Quinn, *Beyond Civilization: Humanity's Next Great Adventure*, New York: Harmony Books, 1999. Personal correspondence.
8. Ibid.
9. Reinhold Niebuhr. "The Serenity Prayer." *http://skdesigns.com/internet/articles/prose/niebuhr/serenity_prayer/*
10. Seth Godin, *Tribes: We Need You to Lead Us*, New York: Penguin.
11. David Korten, *The Great Turning: From Empire to Earth Community* (San Francisco: Berrett-Koehler, 2006), 20.
12. Ervin Laslo, *WorldShift 2012: Making Green Business, New Politics, and Higher Consciousness Work Together*, Rochester, Vermont: Inner Traditions, 2009. Personal correspondence.
13. Thomas Berry. "The Dream of the Earth." *www.ecobuddhism.org/wisdom/thrangu_calligraphy_berry_text/*
14. Sam Keen, *Fire in the Belly: On Being a Man*, New York: Bantam, 1991, 119.

Chapter 10

1. National Institute of Diabetes and Digestive and Kidney Diseases, *www.niddk.nih.gov/health-information/health-statistics/Pages/overweight-obesity-statistics.aspx*
2. Daniel Quinn, *Beyond Civilization: Humanity's Next Great Adventure*, (New York: Harmony Books, 1999), *www.goodreads.com/work/quotes/91355-beyond-civilization-humanity-s-next-great-adventure*
3. Alice Park, "Feeling Alone Together: How Loneliness Spreads," *Time Magazine*, December 1, 2009, *http://content.time.com/time/health/article/0,8599,1943748,00.html*

4. Centers for Disease Control and Prevention, "Insufficient Sleep is a Public Health Problem," *www.cdc.gov/features/dssleep/*

5. Ibid.

6. David Katz, M.D., "Six Habits That Can Add Years to Your Life," *Huffington Post,* June 27, 2011, *www.huffingtonpost.com/david-katz-md /healthy-lifestyle_b_884062.html*

7. Dean Ornish, M.D., "5 Tips for Healthy Weight Loss," *Ornish Living, www.ornish.com/zine/eat-weigh-less/*

Chapter 11

1. Nancy Kalish, "Late-Life Remarriages: The Second (or Third) Time Around," *Psychology Today, November 21, 2011, www.psychologytoday .com/blog/sticky-bonds/201111/late-life-remarriages-the-second-or-third -time-around*

Chapter 12

1. John L. Petersen, *A Vision for 2012: Planning for Extraordinary Change,* (Golden Colorado: Fulcrum Publishing, 2008), *www.arlingtoninstitute .org/fe-archive-volume-11-number-17*

2. John Jeavons, *www.johnjeavons.info/worldofhope_episode2.html*

3. John Jeavons, "Biointensive Sustainable Mini-Farming," *https:// biointensive.net/uploads/pub/media/13/Biointensive_Sustainabe_Mini -Farming__JSA_Article_-Parts_I-V__300_dpi_.PDF*

4. John Jeavons, *www.growbiointensive.org/*

5. Personal communication.

6. *www.johnjeavons.info/john-jeavons.html* and personal communication.

7. Abby Ellin, "After Online Dating, Online Making Up," *New York Times,* March 10, 2014, *http://well.blogs.nytimes.com/2014/03/10/after -online-dating-online-making-up/?_php=true&_type=blogs&_r=1*

8. Personal communications.

9. Ibid.

10. Malidoma Somé, "The Old Must Live in the Young," *http://friends ofsilence.net/quote/1998/10/old-must-live-young*

11. Personal communication.

12. Greg Millan, *Men's Health & Wellbeing: An A-Z Guide,* Haberfield NSW, Australia: Longueville Books, 2010.

13. Ibid.

14. David L. Katz, "What Really Kills Us," *Huffington Post,* November 11, 2013, *www.huffingtonpost.com/david-katz-md/chronic-disease_b_4250092 .html*

15. David L. Katz, MD, MPH, *Disease Proof: The Remarkable Truth About What Makes Us Well,* New York: Hudson Street Press, 2013.

16. Catherine's website: *http://cuisinicity.com.*

17. Personal communication.

BIBLIOGRAPHY

These are the resources I've found most helpful and which I highly recommend you check out for further reading.

Arrien, Angeles. *The Second Half of Life: Opening the 8 Gates of Wisdom.* Boulder, CO: Sounds True, 2005.

Asatryan, Kira. *Stop Being Lonely: Three Simple Steps to Developing Close Friendships and Deep Relationships.* Novato, CA: New World Library, 2016.

Baron-Cohen, Simon. *The Essential Difference: The Truth About the Male & Female Brain.* London: Penguin, 2007.

Bloch, Lisa Friedman, and Kathy Kirkland Silverman. *Manopause: Your Guide to Surviving His Change of Life.* Carlsbad, CA: Hay House, 2012.

Brizendine, Louann. *The Male Brain.* New York: Harmony, 2011.

——— *The Female Brain.* New York: Harmony, 2007.

Buettner, Dan. *Blue Zones: Lessons for Living Longer From the People Who've Lived the Longest.* New York: National Geographic, 2010.

Cacioppo, John, and William Patrick. *Loneliness: Human Nature and the Need for Social Connection.* New York: Norton, 2009.

Callander, Meryn G. *After His Affair: Women Rising from the Ashes of Infidelity.* Ashville, NC: Akasha Publications, 2014.

Campbell, Joseph. *The Hero's Journey: Joseph Campbell on His Life and Work.* Novato, CA: New World Library, 2003.

Cetel, Nancy. *Double Menopause: What to Do When Both You and Your Mate Go Through Hormonal Changes Together.* New York: Wiley, 2002.

Costa, Rebecca. *The Watchman's Rattle: A Radical New Theory of Collapse.* New York: Vanguard Press, 2012.

Crenshaw, Theresa L. *The Alchemy of Love and Lust: Discovering Our Sex Hormones and How They Determine Who We Love, When We Love, and How Often We Love.* New York: Gallery Books, 1997.

Dabbs, James McBride. *Heroes, Rogues, and Lovers: Testosterone and Behavior.* New York: McGraw-Hill, 2000.

Diamond, Carlin. *Love It, Don't Label It: A Practical Guide for Using Spiritual Principles in Everyday Life.* Willits, CA: Fifth Wave Press, 1985.

Doty, James R. *Into the Magic Shop: A Neurosurgeon's Quest to Discover the Mysteries of the Brain and the Secrets of the Heart.* New York: Avery, 2016.

Dowd, Michael. *Thank God for Evolution.* New York: Plume, 2009.

Faludi, Susan. *Stiffed: The Betrayal of the American Man.* New York: William Morrow, 1999.

Fisher, Helen. *Anatomy of Love: A Natural History of Mating, Marriage, and Why We Stray.* New York: W. W. Norton, 2016.

Gibran, Kahlil. *The Prophet.* New York: Alfred A. Knopf, 1923.

Godin, Seth. *Tribes: We Need You to Lead Us.* New York: Portfolio, 2008.

Gottman, John. *What Makes Love Last? How to Build Trust and Avoid Betrayal.* New York: Simon & Schuster, 2012.

Gray, John, Marc Gafni, and Warren Farrell. *Beyond Mars and Venus: The Power of Evolutionary Relationships.* Dallas, TX: BenBella Books, 2016.

Gurian, Michael. *Lessons of Lifelong Intimacy.* New York: Atria, 2015.

Hartmann, Thom. *Walking Your Blues Away: How to Heal the Mind and Create Emotional Well-Being.* South Paris, ME: Park Street Press, 2006.

Hendrix, Harville, and Helen Lakelly Hunt. *Making Marriage Simple: 10 Relationship Saving Truths.* New York: Harmony, 2013.

Jamison, Kay Redfield. *An Unquiet Mind: A Memoir of Moods and Madness.* New York: Vintage, 1996.

Jampolsky, Jerry. *Love Is Letting Go of Fear.* Berkeley, CA: Celestial Arts, 2010.

Jeavons, John. *How to Grow More Vegetables (and Fruits, Nuts, Berries, Grains, and Other Crops) Than You Ever Thought Possible on Less Land Than You Can Imagine.* Berkeley, CA: Ten Speed Press, 2012.

Johnson, Stephen. *The Sacred Path: The Way of the Spiritual Warrior, Journey to Mindful Manhood.* Los Angeles: Sacred Path Press, 2012.

Joiner, Thomas. *Lonely at the Top: The High Cost of Men's Success.* New York: St. Martins, 2011.

Katz, David. *Disease Proof: Slash Your Risk of Heart Disease, Cancer, Diabetes, and More by 80%.* New York: Plume, 2014.

Korten, David. *The Great Turning: From Empire to Earth Community,* Sterling, VA: Kumarian Press, 2007.

Kübler-Ross, Elisabeth. *On Death and Dying: What the Dying Have to Teach Doctors, Nurses, Clergy and Their Own Families.* New York: Scribner, 2014.

Laslo, Ervin. *WorldShift 2012: Making Green Business, New Politics, and Higher Consciousness Work Together.* Rochester, VT: Inner Traditions, 2009.

Legato, Marianne J. *Why Men Never Remember, and Women Never Forget.* Emmaus, PA: Rodale, 2006.

Locke, John L. *Duels and Duets: Why Men and Women Talk So Differently.* Cambridge: Cambridge University Press, 2011.

Love, Patricia. *The Truth About Love: The Highs, the Lows, and How You Can Make It Last Forever.* New York: Fireside Book, 2001.

Love, Patricia, and Steven Stosny. *How to Improve Your Marriage Without Talking About It.* New York: Harmony, 2008.

Martinez, Mario. *The MindBody Code: How to Change the Beliefs That Limit Your Health, Longevity, and Success.* Boulder, CO: Sounds True, 2014.

Millan, Greg. *Men's Health & Wellbeing: An A–Z Guide,* NSW Australia: Longueville Books, 2010.

Moss, Michael. *Salt, Sugar, Fat: How the Food Giants Hook Us.* New York: Random House, 2014.

Munson, Laura A. "Those Aren't Fighting Words, Dear." *New York Times,* July 31, 2009.

Nakazawa, Donna Jackson. *Childhood Disrupted: How Your Biography Becomes Your Biology and How You Can Heal.* New York: Atria, 2015.

Ornish, Dean. *The Spectrum: A Scientifically Proven Program to Feel Better, Live Longer, Lose Weight, and Gain Health.* New York: Ballantine Books, 2008.

Page, David C. *Why Sex Really Matters.* TEDX Beacon Street, https://www.youtube.com/watch?v=nUcgD5DpVlQ, 2013.

Perel, Esther. *Mating in Captivity: Reconciling the Erotic and the Domestic.* New York: Harper Perennial, 2007.

Pransky, George. *Divorce Is Not the Answer: A Change of Heart Will Save Your Marriage.* Blue Ridge Summit, PA: Tab Books, 1990.

Pratt, George, and Peter Lambrou. *Code to Joy: The Four-Step Solution to Unlocking Your Natural State of Happiness.* New York: Harper Collins, 2012.

Quinn, Daniel. *Beyond Civilization: Humanity's Next Great Adventure.* New York: Broadway Books, 2000.

Quinn, Daniel. *Ishmael: An Adventure of the Mind and Spirit.* New York: Bantam, 1995.

Shenk, Joshua Wolf. *Powers of Two: How Relationships Drive Creativity.* New York: Houghton Mifflin Harcourt, 2015.

Solomon, Andrew. *The Noonday Demon: An Atlas of Depression*. New York: Scribner, 2015.

Sutherland, Amy. *What Shamu Taught Me About Life, Love, and Marriage: Lessons for People from Animals and Their Trainers*. New York: Random House, 2009.

Van Der Kolk, Bessel. *The Body Keeps the Score: Brain, Mind, and Body in the Healing of Trauma*. New York: Viking, 2014.

INDEX

ABOUT THE AUTHOR

Here are few things about me that aren't obvious from my work and life experience:

1. I grew up in the San Fernando Valley in California when there were still open spaces and citrus orchards spread out as far as the eye could see.
2. I love romantic movies and imagined myself in films like *Three Coins in the Fountain, Love Is a Many Splendored Thing, High Noon,* and *From Here to Eternity.*
3. I watched *Your Hit Parade* every week on T.V., had a crush on Cheryl on the *Mickey Mouse Club,* and was at Disneyland on opening day, July 17, 1955.

I am the founder/director of MenAlive, a health program that helps men, and the people who love them, to live well throughout their lives. I write books to make sense of my life and to help others dealing with similar issues including the following:

Inside Out: Becoming My Own Man (Fifth Wave Press, 1983)
Looking For Love in All The Wrong Places: Overcoming Romantic and Sexual Addictions (G.P. Putnams, 1988)

The Warrior's Journey Home: Healing Men, Healing the Planet (New
   Harbinger, 1994)
Male Menopause (Sourcebooks, 1997)
Surviving Male Menopause (Sourcebooks, 2000)
*The Whole Man Program: Reinvigorating Your Body, Mind, and
   Spirit After 40* (John Wiley & Sons, 2002)
*The Irritable Male Syndrome: Understanding and Managing the 4
   Key Causes of Depression and Aggression* (Rodale, 2004)
Male vs. Female Depression: Why Men Act Out and Women Act
   (Verlag, 2009)
*Mr. Mean: Saving Your Relationship from the Irritable Male
   Syndrome* (Numina Press, 2010)
MenAlive: Stop Killer Stress with Simple Energy Healing Tools (Fifth
   Wave Press, 2012)
Composting Abbie: A Whale of a Story (Fifth Wave Press, 2014)
*Stress Relief for Men: How to Use the Revolutionary Tools of Energy
   Healing to Live Well* (North Atlantic Books/Random House,
   2014)

You can find my blogs at:
MenAlive, *http://menalive.com/the-blog/*
Huffington Post, *www.huffingtonpost.com/jed-diamond/*
ThirdAge, *http://thirdage.com/authors/jed-diamond-phd-lcsw/*

Good Men Project, *http://goodmenproject.com/author/jed
   -diamond-ph-d/*
National Association of Baby Boomer Women, *http://nabbw
   .com/tag/jed-diamond/*

You can connect with me here:
On my website: *www.MenAlive.com*
Twitter: *https://twitter.com/menalivenow*
Facebook: *www.facebook.com/Dr.Jed.Diamond*
Facebook MenAlive: *www.facebook.com/MenAliveNow*

I enjoy hearing from people and do my best to answer all
correspondence.

this book will be particularly useful to men and women over 40 who want more joy and passion in their relationship as they age. I highly recommend it."
—Michael Dowd, author of *Thank God for Evolution*, and host of "The Future Is Calling Us to Greatness"

"Raw with honesty, deeply compassionate and wisely human, Jed Diamond's new book delivers a road map to help any midlife couple find the love they long to have."
—Donna Jackson Nakazawa, author of *Childhood Disrupted*

"Now is the time to improve your marriage—find out how in *The Enlightened Marriage*. This is a wonderful book, perfectly practical and fun to read."
—Paul J. Zak, PhD, author, *The Moral Molecule*

"Wow! I just finished Jed Diamonds' new book, *The Enlightened Marriage*, and I feel hopeful and empowered. Diamond's new work creates a map for an inspired, dynamic future of expanding intimacy and love."
—Dr. JF Ellington, author of *Slippery When Wet*

"Use this book as a foundation to build a house of lifetime love in your own relationship."
—Lion Goodman, co-founder, Luminary Leadership Institute, author, *Creating On Purpose*

"Jed Diamond has written a beautiful and deeply honest book. So often we think of love as a pleasant or euphoric feeling that comes over us, Jed offers us an alternative—that love is something we can practice, something we can become more accomplished at every day. Everybody will benefit from this book."
—Arjuna Ardagh, co-author, *Conscious Men* and *Better Than Sex*

"I loved reading this book. Through the lens of Diamond's '5 Stages of Marriage' I was able to put my mind, body, and heart fully back where they belong... in love with my wife of 28 years."
—Barry Friedman, one of the four-time World Juggling Champion Raspyni Brothers, and author of *I Love Me More Than Sugar*

"*The Enlightened Marriage* provides the wise guidance needed now to help you navigate the full length of your spiritual journey as a couple."
—Stephen J. Johnson, PhD, author of *The Sacred Path* and *Journey to Mindful Manhood*

"In this beautiful book, Jed Diamond conjoins the strength we derive from our most intimate and important relationship with our capacity to cultivate purpose and meaning, and pay our passions forward. This rendering takes 'doing well by doing good' to a whole new level, and we are honored to figure in the telling of it."
—David Katz, MD, MPH, director, Yale University Prevention Research Center and Catherine S. Katz, PhD, founder *Cuisinicity.com*

"If you breathe air and have a prefrontal cortex (i.e. you're human), this should be required reading. To our brains, every issue is a relationship issue on a continuum from 100% love to 100% fear. In other words, fix your relationship issues and you fix every issue. Dr. Diamond's new book, *The Enlightened Marriage,* is a wonderful guide for healing."
—Alexander Loyd, PhD, ND, number-one international best-selling author, *The Healing Code* and *The Love Code*

"Understanding the five dynamic stages of your relationship can save your sanity as well as your marriage. Jed Diamond applies 40 years of wisdom to help you find real remedies and relief for the real-life issues all couples must face. This is a must-read. Get a copy for yourself and your partner."
—Pat Love, EdD, co-author, *You're Tearing Us Apart*

"The Enlightened Marriage does more than inspire us with the power of two. It gives us concrete tools such as reframing incompatibility as an opportunity to deepen love; recalling traumas of the past to clarify the real challenges of the present, thus deepening our love rather than repeating another journey from 'in love' to losing love."
—Dr. Warren Farrell, author, *Why Men Are the Way they Are* and *The Myth of Male Power*

"The Enlightened Marriage is a compassionate and powerful guide to making a marriage last. Dr. Diamond enlivens the science of marriage with very readable language and wraps his wisdom around case studies gleaned from his decades of clinical experience with couples. I highly recommend this book."
—Michael Gurian, author of *Lessons of Lifelong Intimacy* and *The Wonder of Aging*

"Jed Diamond explains in crystal clear detail how marriages that look to be crumbling can instead be put on a new, vastly improved footing. Don't drop out of your marriage—opt for renewed, lasting love instead!"
—Eric Maisel, PhD, family therapist, author, *20 Communication Tips for Families*

"The Enlightened Marriage offers practical and inspiring guidance for achieving mutually enhancing, sustainable intimacy. While people of all ages will benefit,